MAKE
YOUR
MOVE

CHARTING YOUR POST-MILITARY CAREER

GENE MORAN

LEGACY
launch pad
PUBLISHING

ISBN: 978-1-951407-78-0 e-book

ISBN: 978-1-951407-80-3 paperback

*To the men and women who choose to serve in the
United States armed forces and the families upon which
they rely for ongoing support.*

DISCLAIMER

This work is non-fiction and, as such, reflects the author's memory of the experiences.

CONTENTS

INTRODUCTION

The one certainty for those who serve in the armed forces is that they will one day leave the service. It's as certain as death and taxes.

As a young ensign, I recall a warrant officer telling me that as an officer, I was "part of a 30-year single-elimination tournament," and if I didn't become chief of naval operations, I'd lose. He then took another long drag on his cigarette and laughed uproariously, nearly choking on his own phlegm.

I chuckled nervously. I wasn't a lifer; I joined for the opportunity to gain early professional experience, planning to quickly proceed to the world of business. Twenty-four years later, after a thoroughly exciting career culminating in the command of ships, I left the Navy.

We all get out. It's just a matter of when and how. Then the question quickly becomes, "What's next?" We typically turn to other former service members to help answer this question, but they may not be the best people to ask. It may be time for you to find new mentors and guides. Reading this book, you'll come to see why.

I have clients that pay me tens of thousands of dollars to provide ongoing counsel specific to their business and federal engagement. I've built a seven-figure business based on my broad experiences in military service. But if I offered to counsel a transitioning or newly retired military member toward a fulfilling and profitable postmilitary career for less than $1,000, nearly all of them would be uncomfortable paying that fee.

What's the difference? Why would one group willingly pay so much while the other is reluctant to part with a smaller amount to invest in themselves? The answer is simple. People with military backgrounds generally don't spend frivolously, especially on themselves. Despite our service to a higher purpose and our worldly experience, members of the military tend to have a narrow perspective on their own possibilities. Failure to invest in yourself can inhibit your potential in your postmilitary career choices. It affected me, and I want you to benefit from what I have learned.

Career military people don't serve for financial gain. The nobility of purpose and ongoing fulfillment of military service bring incredible satisfaction beyond money. Those who build long-term military careers have invaluable experience to provide employers and could likely demand large salaries in the corporate world—but they choose to serve. Living with less than others is simply a way of life for military families. The sense of sacrificing for the greater good of the country bears its own reward.

This book is intended to give back to the military community in which I served. I hope to convey lessons by opening up a bit and sharing some not-so-public details of my career that can save you years of frustration and accelerate your path forward. Another form of the give-back is my plan to provide 100 percent of the profits of this book to a great organization, Freedom Fighter Outdoors. I'll talk more about it later in the book, but I want you to see up front that this book really isn't about me; it's about you and others who will walk this path after us.

If you have already left the service and are navigating your next career steps, this book is a great place to start. When service members transition from the military, they need to understand how to correctly leverage their experience into industry. It's common for former military personnel to struggle to fully adapt in the early years of their new civilian careers. They often need help to navigate the culture change they will be experiencing. They are used to a certain orderliness and to training and becoming an expert at a particular job. In both entrepreneurship and corporate life, the path forward is not always linear or clearly defined.

It takes some people years to figure out how to

replace the pride and satisfaction of military service in their lives. It doesn't have to. Failing to recognize the root cause can weigh an individual down, inhibit professional and personal growth and contribute to general unhappiness. I'm not talking about limitations on success in terms of getting a job or jobs in your next career; the overwhelming majority of veterans do find work that pays well. But I'm speaking specifically about fulfillment in the work.

Military members often reach out to me when they're struggling to find fulfillment. Their individual stories share so many common themes that I'm convinced some of them are universal. I've also advised enough corporate clients and leadership teams to see that military retirement shares many attributes with corporate and life transitions. For example, all include elements of planning, self-assessment and mentorship. Developing these skills is vital for a growth mindset. I have devoted a chapter to each principle I believe is key to a successful transition.

Throughout each chapter in this book, I recall stories that illustrate the concepts that guided my various transitions. The lessons can be read as part of my whole story or as a stand-alone resource. While I would like you to read the entire book, if you prefer to go directly to the chapter that best applies to your current situation, permission granted!

I have learned that all difficult transitions offer opportunities that can be used to your advantage. Not all the stories in this book make for glossy Facebook posts; I'll reveal some warts because I want you to relate. My goal is for you to recognize that your story is meaningful, even if it doesn't necessarily unfold as a storybook. We all have a unique path and our own priorities and values that guide us. Recognizing how to make your move will look different for you than it did for me, but I think the common themes hold true for all transitioning military members.

Over the years, people transitioning out of the military have regularly asked me how I made the decision to retire from the Navy when I did, how I made the choice to pursue a corporate role or had the courage to leave the corporate world and work for myself. This book is designed to answer those questions and share what I've learned. Along the way, there are stories of my service and moments that shaped my life. I'm not sharing these because I think my experience is unique. All members of the military have memorable career moments, family members who influence them, seniors in service who looked out for them and favorite songs that represent meaningful moments. These are just mine.

Without these hard-won experiences, my post-Navy career would probably look and feel quite average and yet be characterized as "successful" by almost anyone. Safe in a role with limited challenge, making enough money to live quite comfortably, reflecting on the excitement of my active duty and planning for a time when workdays would be in the rearview mirror. I've come to completely rethink how retirement looks.

I think you should as well.

If you'd like to talk to me about your transition experience and join one of my periodic group sessions on transition success, email me at gene@ capitolintegration.com with the subject line MAKE YOUR MOVE.

MAP THE WAY

"Don't spend too much time in the school of hard knocks. Get your knowledge from reputable resources, not trial and error." -GM

My mom's brother—my Uncle Jack—was a legend in my family.

He was born in 1921 and emigrated from Scotland to the US at the age of four with my maternal grandparents. That part of my family settled in Boston and built a life where 13 years later, my mother was born. Jack and his older brother, my Uncle Jim, both made the family proud with service in the Navy during WWII. Jack was a fighter pilot who served aboard the aircraft carrier USS *Hancock*. Upon returning home from duty overseas, Jack found an entry-level position at a large Boston insurance firm, coincidentally called the John Hancock Company. He worked his way up to chairman and guided the company through its major transition into financial services during the 1980s.

When I was growing up, Uncle Jack's trajectory made a huge impact on me. It became my very definition of success: serving our country and then applying himself to reach the top of the business world. This immigrant experience of the American dream was a vivid example of the possibilities our country offered.

My father served in the Navy during the Korean War where he was stationed on a destroyer escort, the USS *Zellars*. His ship was named for Lieutenant Thomas Zellars, who lost his life in a shipboard fire in 1924 after heroically saving many of his shipmates (and the ship itself) from total destruction. A large painting of that ship hung on a wall in our home. It was a symbol of courage and selfless service and was a part of who my father was in my eyes.

Today that painting remains in my home, reminding me of an important link with my father.

What my dad learned in the Navy had a significant impact on his success that followed. He built a career in marketing with IBM in the 1960s and 1970s. In the mid-1970s personal computers were on the rise. His job led us to relocate from Connecticut to Florida in 1975, when I was 13—a major disruption for the family but one that offered me many new opportunities. As my dad's career flourished, using lessons he'd gleaned from serving our country, I switched to a private high school in Fort Lauderdale, competed on the swim team and learned to sail. Florida exposed me to a different life-style. Most importantly, I discovered my love of sailing and developed a lifelong passion for boating.

Not realizing I was following in Dad and Uncle Jack's footsteps on my way to the Navy, I spent as much time as I could around boats, especially sailboats. I was fascinated by the complex systems of organization that worked together to make a boat sail. My dad understood sailing, having learned it in college. It was a shared interest, although our family did not own a boat. My dad encouraged me to work in a local marine store after school, where I was exposed to countless boat owners and the never-ending repair and maintenance needs of their boats. It was a great job and led to new growth opportunities, which was probably exactly what my dad had in mind.

Many years later, nothing forced me to grow more than supporting my parents during failing health and end-of-life care. Facing these challenges caused me to reflect more deeply on the direction of my own life. The conclusions I drew helped shape this book.

Most of us enter a phase between age 40 and 60 where we are pulled by two generations. Our children and our parents both need us, sometimes in strikingly similar ways. The challenge of supporting and helping others can be both stressful and rewarding. I don't claim to be a counselor to the myriad interpersonal dynamics of families, but I have seen many families experience this phenomenon. As we mature, it's a marker of growth to eventually consider where and how you will spend your remaining working years.

We have all seen people taken too early for any number of reasons: illness, accident, warfare or even a criminal act. None of us believe it can happen to us.

The brilliant leadership coach Dan Sullivan, who has written many books on entrepreneurship, asks a question of his audiences: "How many years will you live?" When pressed, most come up with an answer.

He digs further: "Now when you imagine yourself one year before that final year, will you have done things to take care of yourself? What did that year before look like?" People generally respond that they will be in reasonably good health, have continued with some exercise and maintain a relatively healthy diet.

Dan goes at it again, asking, "Then if you've done these things up to just the year before, would you think maybe you could live longer?" People generally accede to his suggestion. Dan continues, "Since you'll live longer, what's the *real* number of years left?" The audience responds with a new number. In a matter of minutes, he has rationally talked them through adding years to their lives.

My financial advisor employs the euphemism "end of plan" to denote when my financial "plan" runs out. At first, I thought the term was kind of funny. I recently received my annual Social Security "explanation of benefits" that identifies how much I can collect based on when I start to take the benefit. The email from the

Social Security Administration contains a link to an actuarial table that denotes the average lifespan for someone of my present age upon which Social Security has made its assessment of my benefit.

The actuarial table says that if one is 60, the lifespan is one number. But if one is 70, since you made it to that age, your odds have changed somewhat. Well, according to the Social Security Administration, my actuarial date for my eventual passing is several years *before* my "end of plan" for financial planning. That's okay—whatever is left goes to my family, but life doesn't always go according to plan.

My very good friend, Terry O'Brien, an otherwise healthy male, was diagnosed with a serious condition at the end of 2020 and left us within 90 days. He was taken far too soon at age 64. His plans to retire from work, participate on the state senior golfing tour and spend time with family never materialized. Terry served a remarkable career in the Navy, retiring as a captain. He subsequently served our nation in industry, working for two major shipbuilders. He was also chairman of the Shipbuilders Council of America. Anyone who knew Terry appreciated his passion for living, enjoying life and family and doing good work.

My father retired from IBM at age 58. He was downsized out of his position, as IBM and many other companies were struggling to adapt in the 1980s and 1990s. He retired with no idea he would live for nearly another 30 years. He was visibly bored with retirement but didn't have the wherewithal to significantly change his decision. He sought to fill the gap in intellectual fulfillment by teaching adults pursuing their GED. It worked for a time, but I recognize now that his working life could have had another chapter.

My financial planner, the Social Security Administration, life coach Dan Sullivan, my dear friend Terry and my father each had a different answer to the question: "How much time do you have left to work?"

How much time do you have left?

My wife and I live in a beautiful golf community in Florida. Most of my neighbors are retirees or snowbirds who spend part of the year in Florida. A few continue to work from home as part-time real estate agents or consultants. Many have hobbies or play golf two or three times per week. After years in the grind of a structured 9 am to 6 pm lifestyle, the idea of a laid-back retirement was attractive. Now, after realizing entrepreneurship means working on my own terms, the lifestyle of a traditional retirement doesn't appeal to me as it once did. While friendships are wonderful, I now know I would find the lack of intellectual challenge unfulfilling. My perspective from within the constraints of military—and then corporate—life was obscured.

A vibrant consulting career allows me to control my time, choose the companies that I can help, and decide when, where and how I will work. Very little of my work requires hands-on or face-to-face engagement with clients or their customer networks. These relationships give me tremendous freedom of movement and decisions about how my days unfold.

The low-stress work has surely extended my life and makes the idea of working later in life much more appealing. I think very differently about life, about spending and saving, and about how I want to spend retirement than I did when I left the Navy. This perspective on growth might have been helpful at age 40, as opposed to nearly 60, and yet I realize I needed the perspective of a certain number of years to appreciate it. But you don't—you can benefit from my perspective and make your move now.

My peers in Washington, DC, might think I spend my days in Florida polishing my boat in shorts and a Jimmy Buffett T-shirt. And some days that's true, but I still work incredibly hard and deliver results for my clients. Entrepreneurship has offered me the opportunity to apply the best of my natural talents, the skills I acquired in a military career and the tools I have collected in the subsequent years. It has inspired me to develop new skills and seek new knowledge. Charting my own course with creativity and autonomy has become my definition of success.

You never know when you will face challenges that help you grow. I found a way of absolutely thriving in my business in the middle of a global pandemic, but I did this by applying what I've learned through military and corporate experience. I've also made a conscious choice to continue to learn from clients and my own investment in knowledge.

Uncle Jack's example showed me that the Navy could set you up for a successful career in business. My dad's service prepared him to lead our family to a new life in Florida and work in an innovative industry. My passion for sailing helped me understand how leadership and safety go hand-in-hand at sea. Altogether, these things shaped me and led me to chart my course to the Navy, which seemed not only exciting and adventurous but also a proven guide to success. As I started to envision what my life could be, the Navy became my goal.

I served in the US Navy from 1984 to 2008, traveling the world, learning from great leaders, commanding ships, advising senators as well as senior leaders and diplomats. Much like it had for Uncle Jack and my dad, my military career shaped my professional life and gave me a purpose far greater than myself. While I immediately saw the benefit of military structure and the ability to learn through action, it was as I advanced through it that I became aware of the more subtle ways the Navy prepared me to succeed at increasing levels of responsibility.

Still, it was after I retired from the Navy and had been in the corporate world for several years that I learned perhaps the harshest lesson of all. I took what I thought was a steady job upon leaving the Navy; I was a corporate lobbyist. After a little over four years, I was promoted to senior vice president, but within six months and a shuffling of the leadership, my position was redefined: I was no longer needed on the team. Discovering that I was one of those people in the corporate world who loves his company more than the company loves him was a new and unpleasant sensation. I realized then that I was missing a sense of purpose, and working for a large company had been more challenging for me than I was willing to admit. I also began to see my lack of fulfillment for what it was—a failure to invest in myself.

My departure from the corporate world was a critical turning point. Until that point, my rough plan had been to maybe work until 65, then consult as I could before ultimately retiring to a life of leisure. It's what others before me had done, and it seemed a reasonable and secure path. It wasn't until the choice was forced upon me about what to do next that I recognized that I could fill a niche that is staring me in the face. During my time in a corporate headquarters, I learned that there were many people leading companies in industry with a limited understanding of selling to the federal environment. My company supported all of the large prime contractors, and my position gave me visibility on what I would come to know as supply chains and the industrial base. I saw firsthand that many companies downstream in the industrial base had an incomplete picture of their customer and the environment they were selling into.

In the Navy, you learn to "bloom where you're

planted," which just means work hard and stay open to new possibilities. This mindset played a role in helping me identify the opportunity I faced. My corporate counterparts wouldn't be considering retirement for another decade simply to maintain benefits, but military health insurance offers veterans tremendous flexibility. Civilian counterparts are often forced to stay in a bad situation just to hold on to those healthcare benefits for their families. That's not the case with military veterans, yet we don't always take advantage of the freedom to pursue new opportunities while maintaining our benefits.

Why would I want to go to another company, give more years of my life to a corporation and still end up feeling the same way if others chose my fate for me? I decided then that I was going to bet on myself and chart my own course. I would stop following the path of those military members who had gone before me.

I needed to resume command of my own way. I missed the feeling of control that I knew in the Navy. I knew I had the ability to synthesize my experience and offer compelling support and counsel. The Navy taught me how to lead complex organizations and operations.

One evening, as my wife, Julie, and I were discussing options, I admitted the truth out loud, "I think I want to consult."

I knew a few consultants, and I could see myself doing what they did. It looked like something that would offer me the professional control I felt missing.

In Julie's typical selfless style, she supported my proposed new path. As a symbolic first step, she and I established an LLC, Capitol Integration.

Not only was I fortunate to have Julie's vote of confidence, I feel lucky that I was able to recognize why and how to successfully make the transition from the corporate world into entrepreneurship. In pulling the curtain back a bit on my story, I hope to inspire others to consider challenging their own thinking on postmilitary professional life.

There are multiple "right" answers. I hope to help you choose one for yourself.

I did not advance quickly in the Navy and transition from military experience, through the corporate world and then to life as a successful entrepreneur because I'm special. I was an average student, and in most ways, I'm just a regular guy. Yet, I have had incredible opportunities and leveraged those into success in business and life. This is probably why I'm a big Jimmy Buffett fan. His hits like "Margaritaville" and "Volcano" were the soundtrack to my youth in South Florida, and I have followed his career ever since. Buffett's success in five decades of navigating career transitions, overcoming hurdles and turning his passion for singing and playing guitar into a multimillion-dollar empire is the definition of the American dream.

I hope this book will help you define the dream for yourself and recognize your own guides. Finding inspiration in my Uncle Jack's bravery, my father's service and my love of Jimmy Buffett's music is just my story. We each have our own path. And after military retirement, we get to define our own markers for success. My hope is that sharing my story will help you learn from my experiences so you can chart your own course.

The primary thing that sets me apart is my belief in myself and my willingness to continue to grow after the military framework for professional development was removed from my life. I'm convinced every military service member shares the same fundamental attributes of integrity, determination, ability to learn, a willingness to try and the will to persevere. Those are things really anybody can learn.

In the eight years since I started my own business, I have grown exponentially. The success of my business exceeds my wildest dreams. I regularly invest in my professional training, which exposes me to thought leaders and new advisors, and I'm working on my PhD in public policy and administration. I am not the same person I was when I retired from the Navy or when I left corporate America. I am growing at a similar rate that I was when I was on active duty—maybe even more. Maintaining a growth mindset is a key part of fulfillment. Seeing the success of clients who take my counsel and follow my lead is incredibly gratifying. It happens because I have figured out how to bring it all together.

I am convinced any former military member can adapt the experiences I share to chart a course in their own postmilitary career. Nobody's experience is identical, but we share commonalities from years in service that have provided me a valuable perspective. I'm motivated to help because I've been there. We may be retired from service to the military, but we still share the same core values and commitment to this great country. Whether you have completed a military career to retirement or have served a couple of tours before transitioning out, this book is for you.

2

FIND YOUR GUIDES

"When it comes to competition, a healthy amount keeps you motivated and excited." -GM

Some level of fear holds people back from making major career transitions. It can be the insecurity of the paycheck and healthcare benefits, doubt in their ability to make things happen on their own or simply the lack of confidence to jump out of the airplane. Leaving the military is like jumping out of an airplane. You're pretty sure the parachute is going to work, but you have to prepare to make it happen.

My parachute is the structure and principles I learned in the Navy: these have carried me to a level of business success beyond my wildest expectations.

In the military, you learn the value of strong leadership, limits and planning. But the insular culture of the military can make it difficult to consider outside perspectives. Calcified thinking can allow its members to sometimes get stuck. A military person typically can't see this potential fault until they leave the service—if they see it at all. While our networks are geographically dispersed, quite often they are not sufficiently diverse. The people we know well in a professional sense tend to share similar experiences. Seeking new guides and finding people to advise on topics beyond the scope of our military experience is vital to continued growth.

Anyone can learn the ability to always look for the next point of navigation, stay aware of their surroundings, take measured risk and execute quickly. You don't always need perfect solutions—"good enough" will do. And if something isn't working, you need to trust yourself to move on. We must learn to advocate for ourselves after the service and not rely on our next assignment or set of orders for direction. But too often we wait. We wait for an external event to force a change that we could (and maybe should) have made sooner.

This book contains stories of the guides that shaped my life. It also outlines principles you can apply to succeed in any transition. It's not a checklist. It's not a "how to" book. Think of me more like a shipmate, exposing learning points for you to examine and, where appropriate, consider in your own situation.

* * *

I learned as a young man that military service inspires in its members three important skills: courage, competition and coordination. I was lucky to have guides who demonstrated these principles in action early in my life.

I learned the most significant lesson about courage from Uncle Jack.

He and my Aunt Barbara had four kids, my cousins. My cousin Brian was very close in age to me, despite the difference in our parents' ages. As young adults, my cousin Brian and I shared relationship-defining "Dad" stories from our early years during a visit. Brian told me about a conversation he had with his dad when considering starting his own business.

Until that point, Brian had been in the corporate world, and as he outlined his plans to his father, my Uncle Jack remarked on certain aspects, pointing out the associated risks. Brian wasn't hearing what he wanted, and after Uncle Jack referenced a statistic about the failure rate of new business startups, my cousin ended the conversation. He told my uncle he appreciated the input but felt that he'd taken a pretty low-risk path professionally, working his way up at John Hancock. Brian told his dad he was willing to put more on the line. That's when Uncle Jack shared how he developed true courage.

He told my cousin that during his time serving on aircraft carriers in WWII, about 30 percent of the pilots that took off didn't come back. The pilots were required to summon the courage to face their fears and do their duty for their country despite the odds. My uncle learned to watch his fellow airmen leave, knowing many would not return. He developed the courage to keep going each day.

That was a searing memory for me, and though WWII was already far in the past, I realized that war shaped my family. As an adult, I became someone who credits Jack's Navy experiences, especially during wartime, for his courage.

My father routinely referred to his Navy experience during wartime as something he valued because he participated in something bigger than himself and had something to show for it. At an early age, I knew I needed to at least try the Navy and see if it did the same for me. I was guided by the idea of facing my personal fears or discomfort for the greater good.

I was inspired early in life by the courage of the Navy men in my family, and I met more along the way. And there was one who taught me about the importance of competition and coordination more than any other.

* * *

Captain Jim was a reserve Navy captain, airline pilot and real character who was somewhat famous in South Florida sailing circles. I had heard about how he successfully landed a hijacked commercial flight years before. He also owned multiple large racing sailboats and had a regular crew for racing.

Without my knowledge, my boss at the marine store had suggested to Captain Jim that I could crew for him if he needed me. One day while I was working, the phone rang. My boss answered, and I heard him greet Captain Jim familiarly. He was quiet for a moment— then he handed me the phone. I was confused.

"He wants to talk to me?" I asked uncertainly as I took the phone. My boss nodded.

Jim greeted me warmly and invited me to crew for him in an upcoming race. I couldn't believe my good fortune. I recognized Captain Jim as an authority on everything I thought was important: Navy life, sailing boats and cheating death.

Jim was even more friendly in person when I showed up at 8 am the following Saturday. I spent an exhilarating day on the water, racing at a level I had not previously experienced. I was completely hooked.

Captain Jim owned several boats, and I later discovered that the first race had been a tryout. Because I had passed, he would let me crew for him occasionally and eventually regularly. As I grew increasingly fascinated by competitive sailing, Captain Jim became a mentor and a friend, allowing me to officially join his crew and teaching me all about racing offshore sailboats. I admired his infectious sense of humor and big, friendly personality. Everybody knew him as a family man with a strong competitive spirit who loved racing.

The more time I spent around Captain Jim, the more I recognized the qualities that made him extraordinary.

He was a Naval Academy graduate and a successful man. He'd spent 20 years as a Navy pilot in the reserves and flew planes for a commercial airline. When I met him, he was still juggling duty as a naval reservist and commercial pilot. To my young mind, he embodied the heroics of the military and the smarts to succeed in the business world just like my dad and Uncle Jack.

Plus, he was cool.

South Florida in the late 1970s was an exciting world of palm trees, steel drums at patio bars, pastel polo shirts and the regular hum of Jimmy Buffett on the radio. Captain Jim was tough, hardworking and serious about safety, but he had a passion for life on the water and a joy for sailing that was inspiring. He and the crew would often share a cooler full of Hamm's beer and stories of their adventures at the end of a long day at sea. I felt lucky to be included.

I learned later that there is a fine line between Hamm's beer and water.

One of my first big sailing races with Captain Jim was from Ft. Lauderdale to Key West. It was an overnight race, which Captain Jim made sure I understood required a different level of preparation than sailing in daylight. I got special permission from my parents to stay overnight on the boat and miss one day of school for the race, which was thrilling for a high school kid.

We were supposed to be a crew of five, including Captain Jim's wife. A somewhat shady character named

Rob, who had a reputation for being a stellar sailor, was set to be the navigator, a position publicly declared in our boat's race registration. But when the time came to cast off, Rob wasn't there.

I recall Captain Jim checking his watch one last time and then declaring, "Rob has officially missed movement."

At the time, I didn't really understand the terminology, but I caught the seriousness from Jim's expression. His reaction made it clear that however unacceptable Rob's disappearance was, the remaining crew would adjust under his leadership. I later discovered that in the Navy, missing movement is a major infraction. We never found out exactly what detained Rob that day, but he turned up a few weeks later with a bullet wound in his arm. I didn't ask questions; there's a reason the hit TV show *Miami Vice* was based in Miami. There was a lot going on in the subculture in those days.

Looking back, I realize Captain Jim's response to Rob's absence was an experienced captain demonstrating the type of agility that comes with years of leadership in high-stress situations. He quickly designated a role for each person on board and established our 24-hour watch rotation, allowing us to coordinate our sleep shifts.

Captain Jim showed everybody the light list—a navigational tool that described landmarks for a trip, including lighthouses, beacons and buoys—that he'd had laminated—laminated, as in sealed in plastic to make waterproof. This was 1980—laminating wasn't something you did easily. This detail indicated a level of concern and preparation from Captain Jim that struck me.

Up until that point, I was vaguely aware of the concept of a light list, which the Navy and Coast Guard use for maritime navigation. Captain Jim went through his list with all of us, identifying the lighthouses and signals we should encounter on the trip. And this was particularly important for staying on course during that race since it would be going through the night. We were still a few decades from GPS being widely available to civilians.

The fact that Captain Jim had identified each lighthouse and landmark and then laminated his light list for that route has always stuck with me. I now understand the level of planning and coordination involved in terrestrial navigation. Captain Jim had done the work in advance that allowed him the freedom to enjoy the journey. I would later learn to do this kind of voyage planning in the Navy, and I still do it for our offshore boat trips to this day.

When my shift came, my job was managing the sails, changing out various configurations as conditions changed. Since we were racing at night, I was in foul weather gear, clipped into a harness and tethered to the deck for safety. It was the first time I raced tethered to the boat, and that dangerous element thrilled me.

I don't think I slept much during the 24-plus-hour

race; mostly I remember screaming down the coast, headed for a weekend in Key West. For a 17-year-old, this was exciting on so many levels, not the least of which was that Key West was kind of a dangerous place to be at that time. It had a reputation for wild nightlife and drug smuggling, drifters, proximity to Cuba, you name it. It was all new and alluring to me.

It was widely reported that Jimmy Buffett was in the race, riding aboard a sailboat named *Ticonderoga*. Jimmy Buffett was early in his career but very well known in South Florida boating circles. The rumor that weekend was that *Ticonderoga* was for sale and Jimmy Buffett was sea-trialing her. To me, the fact he was considering buying that kind of boat was a marker of success and a life well lived—I didn't know at the time he was just 34 years old!

There were boats of different sizes and designs racing together, so they used a handicap system to rank the race results. The boats are given ratings determined by measurements of hull and sails, their predicted speed or past performance. A boat with a faster rating can give a set amount of time per mile to a slower boat to offset the discrepancy. With a known course, the time each boat takes to sail the exact route is recorded. Then the corrected time is calculated by adding the time allowances to determine an overall winner. In handicap racing, it's possible for the last boat across the finish line to actually win the race.

We crossed the finish line first at the end of the race!

Wind-whipped and sleep-deprived from running on adrenaline, I felt like I'd won a huge victory.

Technically, due to the handicap system, we weren't the winners, but it was still a huge thrill. There were crowds of people waiting at the finish line, and the local news cameras took our pictures. We docked at the naval base in Key West, where all the boats tied up when they arrived. I stayed on the boat with the other crew member, John, after Jim and his wife went ashore to check into their hotel room.

After a day of recovery in Key West, we began to settle the boat for the last night on the island. Earlier we had noticed that a big tent, the type used for outdoor parties, was being set up nearby on the main dock. Now notes from a guitar caught on the wind.

I distinctly remember saying to John, "Listen to somebody trying to play Jimmy Buffett songs."

John was still for a minute and then replied, "That is Jimmy Buffett."

We scrambled and ran toward the music and found a group of about 50 people under the big tent where the beer was flowing, and Jimmy Buffett was on a makeshift stage in front of the group with a guitar. It was like a dream. I was 17 years old, exhausted from the race, sticky from the sea water and suddenly standing in front of one of my heroes. The party wasn't on Captain Jim's light list, but it was the perfect ending to my adventure. That race taught me the value of being prepared, following those with more experience and always staying open to new opportunities.

That's why I've been a Jimmy Buffett fan my entire life.

* * *

The courage, competition and coordination the military inspires in its leaders is something that can stay with us the rest of our life—if we continue to build on it.

Of course, my lessons in these qualities began long before I received an officer's commission in the Navy. Simply witnessing the courage that my uncle and dad had to show up for duty was lesson number one. It sounds simple, but that's when I saw that showing up was the proven way to build sheer grit.

The type of courage that it must have taken Uncle Jack to continue to report to the flight deck each day on the aircraft carrier in WWII, knowing many pilots would never make it back, carried power. The idea that my dad boarded a Navy destroyer during the time of the Korean War, having known of the destroyer losses of WWII and prepared to serve his country with honor, anchored my earliest understandings of courage.

The courage it takes to serve your country is never wasted. It's an investment in the courage of future generations in your family as well as an investment in your own future. There is no substitute for the courage it takes to enlist—whatever your branch, wartime or not.

That same courage is fed by the structure and lessons of military training. It grows and thrives in a system built on preparation. Repetition builds competence. Competence allows courage to flourish—being prepared when your senses are overwhelmed takes courage.

Healthy competition keeps you motivated and excited. The race with Captain Jim was the first time I felt that fire—the thrill of wanting to succeed, sail and win.

The fact that we didn't win the race was a lesson in technicalities. We all knew about the handicapping system, but it didn't matter. I still remember the feeling of satisfaction as we sailed first across the finish line. Facing the challenge was its own kind of success. Rob didn't just miss movement that day; he missed out on a priceless experience.

Of course, the most memorable lesson about coordination for me was contained in Captain Jim's light list. It demonstrated decades of military training coupled with high-level experience in commercial flying. Being coordinated enough to continue that race with a crew of four when Rob missed movement was Captain Jim's vote of confidence in himself as a leader. He knew we could sail safely. He could navigate, but it certainly would have been easier on him with Rob aboard. When he brought us together and showed us the light list, he instilled a sense of teamwork. Nobody is irreplaceable. You fill in and lift your game.

The military offers an amazing path for learning and

moving up but no such clear path for moving out. Each person has to take the lessons from service and make the decision to retire when the time is right for them. How they synthesize the courage, competition and coordination the military teaches will determine their ability to succeed. You've had guides along the way. Will those same guides serve you through this very different transition? This book will help you answer that question.

3

KEEP YOUR FOCUS

"Your time is a nonrenewable resource." -GM

Maintaining focus is vital to any successful endeavor.

In my work as a lobbying consultant, I have the opportunity to counsel business leaders at all stages of the government funding process. There are a million ways to impact those outcomes and help them meet their goal—and almost as many variables at work. One thing I emphasize to all my clients is the importance of maintaining focus on the end goal: getting a government contract. Before we begin, we take the time to get very clear on the objectives. The federal sales process takes time; it's critical that we're on the same page about where the journey together will lead.

Government processes are complex and tangled in procedure—the proverbial "red tape." The bureaucracy exists in the name of saving taxpayer dollars. In this quest to save, we've actually created a monstrous federal acquisition system that costs taxpayers many times what we believe we save. Companies that do not make an effort to understand the various systems within the acquisition landscape will struggle to be successful in selling to the federal government. I often assess their approach and find they're communicating at the wrong place or at the wrong time with their government customer.

For example, if you are attempting to make a change to the budget in the current fiscal year, your effort is likely doomed from the start. Budget priorities are established 12 to 36 months in advance of budget execution. Further, if you go to your member of Congress for help with a problem executing a contract, you will find they can do almost nothing for you. By the time you are in the contract phase, it's too late because you are searching for solutions from the wrong people at the wrong time. Understanding the essence of a situation and taking action at the right time and place are skills that can be applied anywhere.

One of the best lessons I ever got on maintaining focus was when I was still in high school. I regularly sailed in weekend regattas in South Florida with Captain Jim and his family. On this particular day, a Thursday, I was invited to participate in a 60-mile race from Miami to Palm Beach. Boats from all over the East Coast, some with professional crews, came for this event each year. It had a reputation for being a fast race, with crews facing a continuous push of three- to five-knot Gulf-stream currents adding to already-fast racing sailboat speeds.

The boat, an Olsen-30 racing sailboat called *I'm Judy, Sail Me*, was a new design meant to reach top speeds above ten knots, quite fast for sailboats. Since Captain Jim was a commercial airline pilot, it was understood that the boat's name was that of his wife Judy, a nod to the National Airlines practice in the 1970s of naming planes such as *I'm Linda, Fly Me*.

I'm Judy was a recognized competitor in South Florida. As an ultra-light displacement boat, *I'm Judy* could plane on top of the water in certain conditions and surf, where other sailboats displaced water and were limited in their maximum speed.

That day, we recorded speeds of 12 to 14 knots as we raced across eight-foot seas. We wore our harnesses clipped into jack lines that ran along the deck—insurance if we lost our footing. On days like that, Jim was my hero. He had a capacity for excitement and adrenaline tempered with discipline that I found exhilarating. Jim's nerves really were like steel and had been tested many times. After all, he had survived a hijacking as a commercial airline pilot. We knew we were in a competitive boat in conditions that could serve its capabilities.

Aside from Jim and myself, the crew of *I'm Judy* included Tony, a professional sailmaker and John, a regular crew member. John, in his early 20s, was a stellar sailor. The sailmaker Tony was aboard to test the fit of the custom sails. However, he was also an exceptional tactician and was designated by Jim to steer the boat for the tricky start and much of the race. Having him aboard was akin to having a golfer who has played on the PGA tour join your foursome for the company scramble.

My job was foredeck, overseeing the rigging, raising and lowering of the forward sails as conditions changed. I was pretty good at keeping that part of the boat organized. More importantly, as relates to boat speed, I was a somewhat scrawny 140 pounds. Every pound counted when considering weight distribution on the boat.

A few hours into the race, the field had spread out as each tactician gambled how far offshore they could catch the maximum benefit of the current. Ahead of us was a boat everyone knew, the 65-foot *Volcano*, a professionally crewed boat known for its prowess in the venerable Southern Ocean Racing Conference.

Volcano began to visibly struggle with building wind. We all watched in horror as it held its massive balloon-like spinnaker a bit too long and found itself being "knocked down." This is when the boat is laid on its side by wind force, as the keel's weight can no longer keep the boat upright. The boat only rights itself when sails are freed in the appropriate sequence.

Behind us, the fleet looked like a postcard filled with colorful spinnakers dotting the horizon—but we could tell they were struggling. Soon some of them would meet the same fate as *Volcano*, keeping the spinnaker up too long as the wind exceeded the limits of their sails.

In what seemed like seconds later, *I'm Judy* was about to experience the same terrifying fate.

Our professional helmsman, Tony, felt the loss of the rudder's connection to the water—it was now out of the water. Occasionally, that can happen between steep waves. However, in our case, we were sliding down a wave and continuing to heel past 30 degrees, then on to 45 degrees.

His calm words, "I've lost it," remain with me today. I remember thinking, "What does that even mean?" Then I found out, as *I'm Judy* slammed horizontally into the sea, wind and wave conspiring to violently "knock" us down.

I was on the windward rail with my crewmember, John, as this unfolded.

Looking over my shoulder, I watched in mounting panic as our boom, the horizontal stabilizer for the mainsail, snapped like a toothpick. I was amazed at how dramatically, yet matter-of-factly, that piece of equipment failed. To my left, I saw the keel of the boat sticking out horizontally just below the surface of the water. To my right, the spinnaker was tangling with the sea.

We were 10 miles offshore in the heart of the Gulfstream, foundering in a pummeling sea. I knew this was bad, but I didn't exactly know what to do first, let alone what to do.

Luckily Jim did. He efficiently directed recovery actions, shouting above the wind to be heard but not yelling. Firm. Authoritative. "Let's get this unscrewed fast!" kind of shouting. "Release that boom vanguard, release the jib sheets, let's get the spinnaker in first, John—release the spinnaker halyard."

It was a calamity, the likes I'd only read about. There was undoubtedly some paralysis on my part. So many things to be done at once, but I had no idea where to begin.

"She's starting to come back," said Tony.

My job was foredeck, so getting the spinnaker inside the boat was primarily my responsibility, but it took many hands. When it's dry, it practically floats back down to the boat when lowered. When filled with water, it's a hand-over-hand battle to wrench the massive sail from the warm Gulfstream water.

We continued shifting weight to the point of standing on the boat's side—outside lifelines that now served no purpose. Retrieving Tony's custom sails was a huge undertaking, as they were filled with water. We collectively worked to free the boat from the sea's grip. Our cabin hatch had not been closed, as it should have been. Whose job was that? It didn't matter now. Seawater was rushing into the cockpit and was inches from beginning to seep into the cabin. Had that started, the boat would have sunk, as the weight of the water would pull the boat under.

As the sails loosened, the boat climbed back to its

vertical state. The water emptied from the cockpit. The sails were flapping dry, the lines tangled with ripped-out hardware jangling and blowing. As we lowered and stowed the excess sail into the cabin, it hit me.

We were safe.

It was time to assess the damage. We weren't racing. We were recovering, putting pieces back together, and making sense of strewn lines and hardware. The wind and sea had ripped out our normal jib fittings. The boom for the main snapped in half.

"What could we rig as a makeshift to get to Palm Beach?" asked Jim. "There's a finish line up there." Captain Jim was a competitive spirit. That's one reason he was an exciting guy. He had assessed our safety and standing and determined that we still had an opportunity to win the race.

Jim did not lose focus.

I didn't question it. We rigged whatever sails we could to limp across the finish line—as did every other boat. Then, we took a boat hook and strapped it to the boom like a splint. We flew a smaller jib with, shall we say, a "non-standard" connection to the boat. It was a bit of a rig, but we were sailing again. Our sails were rigged in a ramshackle way you will never find in the sailing books, but it was working, and we were making pretty good speed.

We continued across the finish line, placing first in our class. Because our boat had laid on its side for some time, when it came time to start the engine and proceed into the Palm Beach inlet, the engine didn't start. A competitor towed us through the inlet and around the corner to the Sailfish Club in Palm Beach. We were cold, wet and triumphant after finishing a race in such extreme conditions.

As a crew, we had pulled together in a very challenging situation and persevered. This was one of the first times I had triumphed in the face of adversity as part of a team. The feeling of pride it gave me was incredibly satisfying and rewarding, something I had only begun to experience. Jim and the others had been there before.

As we tidied the boat, a club official stopped by to "check on us." He asked to speak to the captain (Jim) or owner and to ask if he could see inside the boat to confirm it had an engine. They knew we had set a record. Because this was a new boat style unfamiliar to the club, and because we came in under tow, suspicions were aroused. They thought we must have stripped the engine out to make that kind of speed.

Boat measurements by which racing boats are handicapped consider the boat's weight when empty. Jim confirmed we had an engine, let the official have a good look and then promptly invited him to leave. He had wrongly challenged Jim's integrity, and that wasn't something Jim took lightly.

I learned that day a great captain can encounter extreme conditions and not only keep the boat intact, the crew safe and follow the rules—he can stay focused and win.

This focused way of thinking has been ingrained in me after years of training to quickly identify problems, process solutions and execute plans. It started in my early sailing experience with Captain Jim and continued to sharpen through the years.

During those teen years, I started planning for a Navy career. The problem with those early plans was that I did not yet see the big picture. I applied to the Naval Academy, inspired by Captain Jim and the other great sailors in my life. It seemed like the natural first step, but I was an average student with no standout qualities—not an ideal candidate. I managed to secure a nomination from my congressman due to a good interview, but I really did not appreciate the competition ahead. At the time I didn't realize that I was competing for a spot at the Naval Academy against other students who had likely been preparing since childhood.

About a year prior to the start of my college application process, my friend and I had raced dinghies at a race held at the Naval Academy. We had gone on to race in California as well.

Based on those experiences, I thought maybe varsity sailing could be a way for me to get into college. I managed to get an interview with the Naval Academy sailing coach, Gary Jobson, of America's Cup sailing fame. After writing him a letter asking for a chance, he quickly replied with a packet of forms, and I flew to

Philadelphia where my grandmother and aunt lived. Together we all drove to Annapolis.

I looked the part walking in, or so I thought. Wearing some brand-new suede topsiders, a preppy Izod polo shirt (popular in the day) and a confident attitude, I walked in all smiles. However, unbeknownst to me, Gary Jobson had moved to a new position, and I found myself facing his replacement.

As I stared at that unfamiliar face, I was completely unprepared for the interview. I now realize I probably looked like a rich kid from Boca with a little too much self-confidence. My interview responses were completely unremarkable. When the coach asked me directly to explain why I wanted to attend the Naval Academy and sail on his team, I was unable to articulate my answer. Having enthusiasm and great desire was not enough.

Unsurprisingly, I was not accepted to the Naval Academy.

With the Navy as my primary focus, I had also applied to both Villanova and Auburn, hoping NROTC might come through. I was accepted to both, but not through the NROTC program. In my parents' eyes, Villanova was a great option because I could live with my grandmother. As much as I loved "Mom Mom," I was like most 18-year-olds, anxious for freedom. Moving from my parents' home to my grandmother's held zero appeal. Auburn was a popular choice for many from my high school, but I knew nothing about

Alabama and really only applied because some of my classmates had.

Florida State was the backup to my backup plan for college, but it was there that I first learned to recognize the importance of looking for signals and opportunities in life. I quickly learned it was possible to enter NROTC as a "walk-on" through the college student program on campus. That's how I found a way into the Navy as a commissioned officer during my first week at Florida State.

I was an academic underperformer while studying political science at FSU. Classes were generally large, and my sense of personal accountability was low. But college life had some benefits because I met my future wife, Julie, at FSU. Talk about learning to recognize valuable opportunities! So, it happened in the spring of 1984 that I graduated with my bachelor's, accepted a commission to the US Navy as an ensign, then married Julie a few months later.

Although I had not yet mastered the concept of planning, I had managed to reach my first few markers of adulthood and get into the Navy. From an inauspicious start, a plan for my professional future was coming together. My Navy career taught me much about maintaining focus in the face of adversity. But one of the first powerful lessons I got about keeping a cool head was from my friend, Captain Jim.

* * *

In March of 1985, I reported to my first ship, the USS *Flatley*, a relatively new ship whose commissioning crew was just beginning to turn over. The experience for me was unimaginably positive because I had great leaders who helped me learn to identify my strengths. My sailing background had taught me the concept of relative motion—how the wind and sea affect a boat or ship. This meant I had an advantage over my fellow ensigns in learning to drive the ship. It was exhilarating to have an opportunity to recognize what I was good at. In the military, you're given a linear path toward progress. It's simple: you either succeed and move up, or you don't succeed and move out. I appreciated the chance for hands-on learning in the Navy after college. This was not a boring office. It was one new experience after another.

I believe your first ship can set the tone for your career in the Navy. I am thankful for the great leaders that guided me in those early years. On that first ship, I had two captains who looked out for me and challenged me with opportunities. There were other great leaders as well, chiefs and lieutenants alike. Although I was inspired by the constant challenges of living and working aboard a ship, I was also facing a period of transition.

I wasn't used to being at sea for extended periods, and my wife, Julie, was pregnant for the first time. Letters routinely took 18 days to reach me, and the fact that I wouldn't be there to share the birth experience with her was a source of ever-present disappointment. I looked to the examples of my superiors for support. One coping mechanism many adopted was listening to music —on cassette tapes. It was common for all of us to copy an original tape to a blank tape to produce a bandit tape of mediocre quality.

My department head knew how to motivate and inspire with humor and grace. At the end of a watch, he came in my room displaying Jimmy Buffett's new release, "Last Mango in Paris," which he had just received in the mail and grinning ear to ear. "Because you're such a good guy, I've made one for you, Parrot-head. Keep up the great work!" In an instant, my spirits were lifted, and an uncommon connection was cemented. The simple gesture had deep meaning in the moment.

Those leaders saw potential in me and embraced my young family and me. When our first daughter, Katie, was born a few months later while I was deployed in the Mediterranean, I was able to fly home briefly. I learned later that this was not common practice and only happened because of a supportive leadership team on the ship.

Another special detail I remember from my first deployment on the USS *Flatley* is that the ship was named for a renowned WWII-era Navy tactician and aviator, Vice Admiral James H. Flatley Jr. After growing up in the shadow of the painting of the USS *Zellars*, hearing stories of torpedoes, kamikazes and bravery during WWII, this bit of trivia was important to me.

In those days, carrier battle groups would meet up to turn over "med duty." Two groups of roughly 15 ships each, including submarines, would join up in a massive formation. Navigating in those conditions requires an extreme level of focus on your own position but also requires a fluid understanding of the vessels around you. I recall being on the bridge as a junior officer of the deck with my department head as the officer of the deck. Our battle group, centered around USS *Saratoga*, was commanded by Rear Admiral James H. Flatley III, the son of our ship's namesake and an exemplary officer in his own right. Admiral Flatley's staff ordered our ship to position front and center and quite close to present a terrific photo op of USS *Flatley* in front of this nearly 30-ship formation commanded by Rear Admiral Flatley. It created a definite stir of excitement aboard our ship and made for a lasting memory.

I didn't need any extra incentive to perform; I was in my element as I tracked the formation of the ships. I scrambled to keep up with the converging dots on the radar scope, using a grease pencil and tongue depressor to track our path and our proximity to other ships as we maneuvered to station. I was completely challenged and engaged, and it was not unusual for a four-hour watch to fly by. I didn't know it, but my performance in such scenarios allowed me to stand out in the eyes of my seniors.

I focused on doing my best and learning everything I could on the *Flatley*, and it paid off. After roughly two years on the ship, I received a phone call on the quarterdeck from my detailer, the person who would administer my next assignment. It was typical to do two division officer tours back-to-back. I expected I would be assigned to another ship. Instead, he presented me with an unexpected opportunity.

"How would you like to get your MBA at Monterey?" my detailer asked.

My mind raced. Monterey is the Naval Postgraduate School at Monterey, California. This C-student was being offered a chance to get a master's degree? The degree was actually an MS in financial management, not exactly an MBA. I talked to Julie about it, and we agreed to jump at the chance.

I thought I could use a master's degree anywhere, whether I stay in the Navy or not. I had no idea at the time, but my captain had an MS in financial management and was a "proven" financial manager in Navy parlance. I didn't realize that the value of such a degree in the Navy increased the more senior I became. This was an opportunity coordinated by my captain. Accepting orders to Monterey would mean an additional service commitment, but it seemed a good trade.

I was given the opportunity to go to Monterey while I was still a lieutenant (junior grade), which, at the time, was uncommon. This was not just a result of my own hard work, although that played a part. My success at that point in my life was because my dad, Captain Jim and my superiors early in my career took the time to guide me. I've never forgotten the many lessons of my first ship. Those learning experiences and guides pointed me in the right direction early in my Navy career.

As I advanced, I learned the value of maintaining focus. In the absence of proper preparation for the Naval Academy, my focus on the Navy had still carried me in the right direction. Once commissioned in the Navy, I realized that learning from respected leaders who had come before me was a proven way to chart a successful course. As I remained focused on my goals, the right guides became clear in my path, leading me to new opportunities.

As you transition through postmilitary opportunities, it can be easy to lose focus. You've learned how to focus throughout your military career but within an organization that knows how to guide a mission and objective. That environment will change as you move out from under the umbrella of military service. Like the vague notion of how many years we have left to live and work, the goals and objectives of our careers may be less clear after military retirement. The good news for you is that the same answer applies here, as well.

It's up to you to make your move.

4

IMPLEMENT PLANNING

"You have settled into roles along the way. Let go of that mindset; you don't have to fit in." -GM

In order to find your next move, you have to stay curious. Try on different skills, different solutions, different paths. In our careers and in life, if we keep doing the same thing over and over, we're bound to get bored or disappointed by the results. The built-in systems for advancement and on-the-job training in the military can foster a growth mindset. I found one of the keys to achieving that level of growth in my postmilitary life and business is my ability to plan. I credit my early years of sailing and my time in the Navy with teaching me how to create and execute plans.

A key part of planning is the ability to assemble the right team for any project. In the military, you are part of a crew (or subset of the crew) or a larger team with a clearly defined role. To transfer that infrastructure to life beyond retirement, I found I needed mentorship or team support. I think we all do.

Sometimes mentorship means seeking a specific type of training or hiring the outside support of experts in an area we may be unfamiliar with. Our first inclination may be to save money and try to go it alone, especially for former military members. Pro tip: invest in yourself. For me, sometimes that means I must commit to educating myself. That growth mindset is what drove me to become an excellent consultant—not just someone who hangs out a shingle. I'll describe later how I've immersed myself in ongoing training to earn that distinction. The growth mindset also drives my progress in my PhD program, my professional development and my desire to continually improve myself.

Having planning processes in place allows you to have many projects or opportunities in motion simultaneously and still finish most of them. This is also how you effectively run a ship. Not every plan will come together, but the process of creating the plan gives you the full picture of your options, which allows you to adjust quickly to whatever happens.

I find immense value in planning in my professional life. Just like Captain Jim's light list, a plan can help you stay on course with larger goals while there are many smaller systems at work behind the scenes. One of my favorite planning tools is a dry-erase board. It's a very visual and tangible reference point. I keep a "light list" on a dry-erase board in my office. It has sections for each of my projects, priorities and goals.

The details in my office light list are minimal, it's a high-level plan, and the specifics live in other documents, but it is enough to keep me on course each day. Some days I have a multipage call list, and some days I don't. But there are always short, medium and long-term priorities and deadlines unfolding. I'm always moving forward because I have built planning and goal setting into my work lifestyle. The most important thing about my dry-erase light list is that it is specific to this time period. Some projects stay on the list for months, even years, but they advance and are eventually replaced by new ones. The priorities on the whiteboard today don't look like those of two years ago.

In two years, the whiteboard will look entirely different because I will be adapting and creating something new.

The Navy emphasizes on-the-job training, requiring that the people in leadership know how to convey the knowledge of their position. When service members retire and enter the corporate world, they can find themselves without a structure in place for mentorship or advancement. They may struggle to grow because they don't realize it is their responsibility to develop and implement their own training plan. In the Navy, we often heard the phrase, "bloom where you're planted." You don't always get your first-choice job or location, but you always have the opportunity to advance. If you want a different job, work hard and make sure people know you want to move up—your superiors will notice. They are trained to see your potential and help you grow. Their growth often hinges on yours.

This isn't necessarily true in corporate America. When you come from the military with an incomplete understanding of the corporate environment, you may find yourself unprepared for the fact you may work for people who don't know what they're doing. Or perhaps they are not as interested in your growth as your military leaders may have been. It is possible to stagnate in the corporate world because the lack of a formal system of advancement can breed apathy. People often get hired from the military for their Rolodex or their perceived "customer" or business acumen, but they don't get properly introduced to the realities of business.

There is a complete shift in culture when you transition from the military to the corporate world. The focus is no longer on readiness nor even on not losing money —it's always about making money. It makes sense and is in most ways obvious. It's the reason companies are in business—to make money. But the cultural shift is enormous.

The military just doesn't think like that.

Mission accomplishment and readiness are paramount. Financial costs are rarely considered. How much is too much to spend? Don't our troops deserve the best training and equipment? Of course, there is no perfect answer to those rhetorical questions. But the emphasis on training, procedure, camaraderie and the "leave no man behind" mentality is a culture not limited by financial constraints. Saving or making money is not part of the military calculus. We hear various companies package their values in different ways—they can call the customers "guests" all day long, but if an initiative doesn't make money, they don't pursue it. If you have an incomplete understanding of this profit-loss culture, you don't know the questions you need to ask to assess a cultural fit with a company. Those cultural cues and barriers can be identified by a savvy mentor or a strong business leader, or you can learn it yourself through trial and error.

It can be challenging to identify former military figures who have achieved the level of success in business they did in their military careers. There are, of course, easily recognizable names of leaders who have done quite well—Admiral McRaven, General Mattis, Vice Admiral Dawson, Admiral Mullen, to name a few. Each transitioned successfully to very high-profile corporate roles commensurate with their deep experience and talent. However, there is a very big gap between a retiring master chief, sergeant major or Navy captain and a four-star admiral or general. Many in between haven't excelled in business the way they did in active duty because they failed to adapt fully and embrace the void they now needed to fill. This is often because they can't see how some of their military training and mindset have held them back in the corporate world.

My present work exposes me to the defense industrial base and the hundreds of companies that make up the supply chains. I meet countless former military members working for corporations, marking time—sometimes underutilized and often personally unfulfilled. The pay is better than they have ever known, but the levels of satisfaction are often palpably low. It doesn't have to be this way. But I've learned that to achieve the same level of professional fulfillment I experienced in service, I must get out of my own way and stop editing my dreams.

There's a tradition in the Navy that goes hand in hand with the idea of blooming where you're planted. This is the idea that if you stay focused but make your desire for advancement known, opportunities come your way. You may not end up with your first-choice assignment, but if you build relationships with your superiors and work hard, doors open.

This was certainly true in my father's Navy career. My father had a chemistry degree from St. Joe's of Philadelphia before joining the Navy to serve during the time of the Korean War. He was made an electrical officer aboard the USS *Zellars*, which was not his first choice—he wanted to be a navigator. Still, he dedicated himself to his assignment as an electrical officer but made it clear to his superiors that he wanted to move up. His captain saw his hard work and drive and was impressed. When the navigator position became available, the captain selected him. His ship served as a flagship for an embarked commodore whose role was to coordinate other ships in a task force. Being navigator exposed my father to the leadership dynamic of his captain, commodore and the other commanding officers of the squadron. It was an eye into the importance of those interrelationships.

This story instilled in me the idea that you should always work hard at the job in front of you but stay ambitious. And I learned to always signal to my superiors that I'm interested in new opportunities because those are always on the horizon.

* * *

During my first tour on the USS *Flatley*, as junior officer of the deck, I enthusiastically plotted our course. After proving myself, I was able to qualify as an officer of the deck during that first Mediterranean deployment and eventually advance to serve as Combat Information Center (CIC) officer. In that role, I was given the opportunity to plan a Caribbean trip for the ship to "show the flag." This planning involves calculating time and distance between ports, consideration of arrival and departure times and training opportunities between stops. It's not particularly difficult, but the idea of staring at a chart of the Caribbean presented a flood of possibilities.

My creative department head wanted to try some new places, and I was eager to get in on the action. We chose Roosevelt Roads, Puerto Rico, which was a regular refueling stop for Navy ships at the time. From our homeport in Mayport, Florida, that was a logical first stop. As we charted the course for the rest of the trip through the Caribbean, I looked at the chart and realized we could stop in both Barbados and the British Overseas Territory of Montserrat. The Soufrière Hills volcano on the island of Montserrat inspired the hit Jimmy Buffett song "Volcano," and I was excited to see it. There were other Jimmy Buffett fans on the ship, and it felt cool to have a hand in directing this particular movement to a port visit. Amazingly, this plan was approved by Navy and State Department officials who track these contacts for diplomatic purposes.

During the visit, I learned that Montserrat not only inspired the song but was also where Jimmy Buffett recorded it. The island was home to the famous British AIR Recording Studio, owned by George Martin, who was a producer for The Beatles. The studio was built in 1977, and Buffett recorded the "Volcano" single there in 1979. During the 1980s, Paul McCartney, Elton John, The Police, The Rolling Stones and many other iconic artists recorded at AIR Studios Montserrat.

Once again, Jimmy Buffett was lighting my way.

My time at the Naval Postgraduate School exposed me to a cohort of classmates who were all older than I. For budget reasons, promotions to lieutenant were delayed by a number of months in late 1987. While I had been selected for promotion, I arrived at Monterey as a lieutenant (junior grade). Because we wore civilian clothes to class, it took a while for my classmates to understand just how junior I was. Julie and I married relatively young. We already had one daughter, with a second due within months of arrival at school. Some may have seen me as more mature than I was. My class leader was a commander—the same rank as my prior ship captains—and the only commanders I knew!

Most of my classmates were at least five years my senior. Personally, that cohort offered support for myself and my growing family. Julie and I welcomed our second daughter, Andrea, while we lived in Monterey. We were both around 25, with two kids, and it was nice to be part of a community of similar families raising young children. Professionally, I had a tremendous pool of mentors ready to share their experiences as ship department heads. They encouraged me to think about my future in the Navy. In the surface warfare community, as you shift into the role of a department head, you are now a company man: the type of service member likely to become "a lifer" who will serve 20 years or more.

* * *

Late in 1989, I was assigned to a ship based in Charleston, South Carolina. I reported for duty just a few days before we received orders to move ships from the port as Hurricane Hugo was bearing down on the East Coast. All the ships that could get underway left port to escape Hugo's path.

As is always the case, families are left behind to fend for themselves. They learn to draw from their own determination and wits and support each other. As a partner and a parent, it's a terrible feeling to leave like that, but as a naval officer, it's the job. When disaster struck, the crew's top priority was to protect the ship from being damaged in port. My crew and the crews of other ships had to take immediate action and work to relocate equipment worth hundreds of millions of dollars, valuable assets of the US government, out of the path of the storm. As crazy as it sounds now, I knew Julie and the families could handle our homes.

The storm foreshadowed a very difficult tour. The ship was poorly organized, probably because the leadership team was not well integrated or aligned. As if to demonstrate this, we failed a ship-wide maintenance inspection and major engineering examination in close order. Morale was low, and we were all miserable.

Then, slowly the key leaders began to turn over.

Fresh blood, innovative thinking and a deployment to the Middle East allowed the ship to change focus and improve itself. This dramatic turnaround was directly attributable to changes in leadership. In some cases, normal rotation and attrition took place. In other cases, difficult decisions needed to be made. The removal of some from their positions was required. When standards are no longer being met, change must be brought to bear. In the military, standards are minimums and are often written in blood.

One of the fresh leaders was our new engineer, Taylor Skardon. He was positive and enthusiastic and knew how and when to use humor to move people. I credit him as the individual who was largely responsible for the changes in the ship. Soon, Taylor's skills were noted, and he was offered an operations officer position on a cruiser by the prospective commanding officer of the new ship. Taylor wanted to be an engineer, but that position was not open.

Knowing I was looking to move, Taylor instead told that captain, "With all due respect, sir, you want Gene Moran if you're looking for an ops officer."

I will never forget when I heard that.

Taylor's genuinely humble and professional gesture changed the trajectory of my Navy career.

Taylor was not the only bright spot in that tour. Julie and I had our third daughter, Jillian, while living in Charleston. Taylor and his wife Nancy also welcomed a child the same year, and we eventually exchanged the honors of serving as godparents to each other's babies. He eventually moved on to an engineer role in another brand-new cruiser, commanded a DDG, rose to the rank of captain and later held major command. Today, Taylor Skardon teaches leadership classes at The Citadel in

Charleston, a perfect fit for a natural mentor and gifted leader.

My next ship, USS *Vicksburg*, was the epitome of a ship well led and well trained from the keel up from day one. I was part of its commissioning crew wherein Navy procedures and training are implemented to that specific ship and crew. This experience became my new baseline of what the "like new" standard of performance for the ship and crew should be. Precommissioning duty is a four-year tour, which begins in a schoolhouse and culminates in a major deployment.

On that ship, two commanding officers and executive officers demonstrated how to set incredibly high standards and strive for seemingly unattainable goals. The environment was competitive, but we drove each other to succeed, and everyone was a winner. Many from that wardroom went on to command their own ships. There were difficult moments, but the success of the ship was well respected by all. I applied the lessons about leadership I learned on the *Vicksburg* aboard my next three ships, two of which I commanded. "Like new" was a phrase and a concept I would take with me.

That difficult tour, which began during the evacuation for Hurricane Hugo, taught me how to welcome new opportunities in the midst of chaos. Until then, my Navy career had been relatively smooth sailing. Encountering an extremely difficult assignment gave me a chance to learn new communication skills. I really had a chance to "bloom where planted" by building relationships with my peers and superiors and gaining valuable support. My family with Julie and our now three daughters was also thriving.

That tour would not have been an incredible learning experience without my own willingness and the peer reference at just the right moment from my friend and shipmate, Taylor.

In 1989 Hurricane Hugo caused major damage to the US East Coast and the Caribbean. The island of Montserrat was devastated, and AIR Studios was destroyed. I feel fortunate to have seen the island when I did. Although that trip was relatively inconsequential in the big picture of my career, it was a guiding light.

5

GET EXPERIENCE

"Competence breeds confidence, and confidence enables courage." -GM

Experience builds confidence. But in the absence of experience in a particular area, knowing your place in the big picture and understanding the possible limitations of your role are keys to success.

Anytime you transition, you may be facing the unknown.

Even when you think you know the lay of the land, many situations look different from within. You may find that you don't yet have exactly the right experience for the new role but have your own toolbox. Each experience you've lived becomes a tool you carry with you for the rest of your life. Some tools work better than others.

Allow yourself a period to recognize which of your

previously developed skillsets might transfer to your new position—and which don't. You might have to learn the language first and figure out where your previous experience will translate before jumping in. Some choose to lay low, wait and watch when arriving somewhere new. Others may overcompensate for their insecurity by bloviating or otherwise marking new turf.

I consider myself an average guy, yet I have had extraordinary experiences and achieved a level of success I could never have imagined. Now I use my experience to advise company presidents and leaders about a world they don't fully understand: the congressional process and the federal buying process. I can explain what's going on within its proper context. Whether it's budgeting, funding, legislation or acquisition, their ongoing effort fits somewhere in this complex process.

I can't always tell my clients when a piece of legislation is going to come through the system. But I show them how it's going to come through in one of these specific ways, and we want to be prepared for any of them. In each case, I am applying decades of experience to a unique set of circumstances and variables—against the backdrop of overarching processes. I own those tools and that skillset. What sets me apart is that I find ways to use my experience to help my clients take advantage of opportunities about to unfold. This is something anybody can learn. Surprisingly, few become experts at it.

In my years of sailing, service and business, I have developed the ability to see the big picture quickly. Situational awareness has become natural—in the military, we call it SA. It was identified through the military challenges and fed by constant opportunities to practice. Connecting the pieces to a common objective has been the core of what I do, and it has translated from one job to another. Most people with military experience share this ability to some degree. Some recognize it. Some don't.

In the military, you are trained continually. Training for the next operation, the next assignment and the next position is fundamental to military service. After retirement from the service, most people fail to see this gap in ongoing learning, sometimes for years. It took me a while to appreciate the deficit for what it is: something within my control.

Investing in our own learning should be a first-order priority upon transition from the military. Many branches of the service have centers of excellence where skills are regularly honed. You don't see that in corporate America—only a very select few get to attend the exclusive schools for executive learning. In corporate life, I rarely see people investing in themselves. It is just not a universal culture the way it is in the military. Many executives have the means, the smarts and the time, but they don't do it for themselves.

When I am coaching people through various transitions, I always emphasize the idea of maintaining a growth mindset. I often meet people who are riding the success of their last few years. Experiencing success is great, but if you're not investing in your own growth, you can't effectively advise others—and you will atrophy. Apathy will follow. It often hits postmilitary people around year three after departure from the service.

I believe this phase of apathy sets in when you recognize that there is not a new set of orders, a next billet or a new challenge around the corner. This can inspire an awakening. This is the cohort of people who approach me most often. They enjoyed a successful career of service. Upon military retirement, they typically take what they think is a great job for nearly double their military salary. But a few years into the new gig, the lack of fulfillment is clear.

My experience has uniquely positioned me to understand this group of people and the circumstances they face. I have lived it. When I was in the Navy, I encountered endless opportunities to learn and grow. If I was passed over for an assignment, I discovered that if I kept my eye on the big picture, there was always another chance.

I understand that building experience creates forward momentum in life. This is ingrained in the military lifestyle. After retirement from service, what's missing for many people is the feeling of possibility that comes with ongoing exposure to new opportunities.

* * *

During my first deployment to the eastern Mediterranean in 1985, TWA flight 847 was hijacked during a routine trip from Athens to Rome. The terrorists on board forced the plane to crisscross the Mediterranean for days, demanding the release of Lebanese from an Israeli prison. The plane landed three times in Beirut, Lebanon, to refuel and exchange hostages.

When this international incident occurred, I had only been deployed for a couple of months. The flow of information was not what it is now—there was no internet, no communicating by email.

I learned during our daily operations briefing that our ship was in the middle of a major news event. It was far above my paygrade to understand the logistics of the incident or the role my ship played in national security on the international stage. However, everyone on the ship was more than casually interested in what was unfolding.

Although I understood academically that we were near the location of the hijacking, I didn't realize we had been positioned there to signal US military presence. Because I had no experience, I was unaware of my role in the bigger picture.

As an ensign with three months on board, I was still learning my way. As I rose in rank, my awareness levels kept pace with the increase in responsibilities. I realized the enormous benefit in always keeping one eye on the big picture. Knowing your position allows you to recognize when you're at the right place at the right time.

With some humility, it can also inform you when your timing is not quite right.

The big picture awareness holds the key to finding new opportunities. You must always maintain SA. Losing SA means people can get hurt or even die.

During the summer of 1995, I was assigned to Naval Military Personnel Command in Washington, DC, as a placement officer for major staffs. After several months, I interviewed to be aide to the vice chief of naval operations, and I was not selected for that position. I'll never forget the graceful letdown by Admiral Prueher, who told me I wasn't "right for the 'mosaic' of the office," which was a reference to my being a surface warfare officer. He chose an aviator for the position. But by then, I had embraced the idea of blooming where I was planted. Soon, I had the chance to interview for the role of deputy flag officer detailer—this time, I was selected. This is the office where admirals are assigned their jobs, and working there provides a global perspective on the senior Navy.

My position offered me a direct view into the process of assigning our most senior officers to the "best fit" leadership roles around the globe. Of course, best fit always depends on the individual, the service need and the timing of rotations. Although I already knew it in an academic sense, this is where I learned not everyone can succeed in every type of job.

This is where I first faced the reality that there comes a time when everyone leaves the service, even the senior-most officers.

During that tour, I sat on multiple flag officer selection boards as one of several administrators of the secret selection. It was another fascinating glimpse of how the highest-ranking officers were evaluated by their seniors for their accumulated skills and talents and how they could best serve the Navy from the top—or not. It was a sneak peek at the importance of developing skills that mattered within a broader context. Although I didn't fully comprehend the impact of that role until years later, I was truly learning through the experiences of others.

Learning from the experiences of those who have come before us is a common practice in service. The systems and hierarchy in place ensure those seeking mentorship will find guidance. This is not necessarily true in the corporate world, and it is certainly not the case for entrepreneurs. After military retirement, it's up to you to find your own examples and learn from them. The fact you have this book in front of you is a good start.

Flag officer detailing was an eye-opening opportunity within the Navy personnel command. It's a nondescript office suite where decisions about admiral staffing are made based on what senior admirals think is the best assignment for a particular person. In that role, I was introduced to how these concepts were evaluated. From that leadership vantage point, it was important to understand the big picture and who would fit best in each position. Skills were an important part, but so were family issues that we knew would impact their performance. I realized that some perform better with a strong supporting cast, even in the military. Others need no such help. Piecing those tidbits together to help identify assignment options was an ever-present part of the detailing calculus.

Surprisingly, I didn't have to sign any NDAs, but understanding how the pieces fit together down to the smallest details is the reality of dealing with the senior leaders of any service. Turns out, it's quite similar in corporate. Do people want to work with you or not? Captain Bob Erskine was my boss at the time. As a man of unparalleled integrity, he made clear to me that we were expected to take some of what we learned to the grave. He wasn't kidding.

While I served under Captain Erskine, one of my collateral roles was to assist with a class for transitioning flag officers called the Career Transition Seminar (CTS). It was a precursor to what is now widely known as the Transition Assistance Program (TAP). It was a five-day workshop, which culminated over a weekend and included both the flag officers and their spouses. It was taught quarterly, and my role was to be a "butt in a seat" representing the office of flag officer detailing. The emphasis the military places on planning extends to offering resources to prepare for military retirement. This class was led by retired Admiral John Ruehlin himself, the founder of this course concept. The education was simply eye-popping for me.

Ruehlin had embarked on a career in the corporate world after retiring from the Navy in 1986. He eventually launched his own business in the early 1990s that offers career management and planning specifically designed for transitioning service members. He is still considered the expert on the topic of retirement planning in the Navy, and the transition courses are still referred to as "the Ruehlin course." What is now commonplace and expected in helping to figure out one's first job after the military is grounded in Admiral Ruehlin's pioneering work of the day.

As a lieutenant commander and deputy flag officer detailer assisting the instructor, I was at a different point in my career than the others taking the class, but I paid close attention. As I watched other Navy couples planning for life beyond the service, I recognized the importance of maintaining SA on a career level and confirmed that, indeed, everyone has to leave the service at some point.

I was particularly interested in the role the spouses played in financial planning and decision-making. Julie and I made decisions as a team. Military families have no direct control over job assignments and deployments, but they are the discreet scaffolding that supports the armed forces. At this point in my career, we had just welcomed our fourth daughter, Rachel. The fact that Julie had navigated multiple deployments, pregnancies and moved our home at least 10 times in our dozen years of marriage was not lost on me.

The Ruehlin course humanized the military retirement process for me. It reminded me that leaving the service involved so much more than the pageantry. I realized Julie and I should always plan to evaluate my career opportunities relative to our financial and geographical positions and our larger objectives. Having this level of exposure to the planning process for military retirement at that point in my career was both a signal of my advancement and a gift of knowledge.

I also picked up a valuable piece of advice from Admiral Ruehlin that I will never forget. At one point during the five-day course, Ruehlin said learning to do things for yourself after years in the military was a basic challenge most retiring service members face. He strongly encouraged all the attendees to go back to their posts and practice tasks like writing their own letters, making their own copies and placing their own phone calls. In the military hierarchy, juniors often perform these duties, but Ruehlin reminded us that doing those basic things well is important in business.

A few days later, I was back in the flag detailing office filing the paperwork from the CTS when I discovered I needed to speak to Admiral Ruehlin. I had a quick question and asked my assistant, a chief petty officer, to get him on the phone immediately, which was a normal course of action in such circumstances—but not with Ruehlin. Not after you did a seminar with him. When he came on the line, he gave me a well-deserved earful about taking responsibility for my own growth and challenging myself to learn something in every situation. At the time, I think we were both slightly amused. After all, I had technically just been a "butt in chair" at the seminar, but it is a lesson in humility and self-sufficiency I have never forgotten.

That assignment was a chance to build my reputation and meet some senior officials who would impact my future. Now, looking back, I realize at that level of my career, there was not much to differentiate one candidate from another when a selection board is reviewing personnel. The fact that somebody may have recognized the name "Gene Moran" and identified me with the office of flag officer detailing built my credibility. In the Navy, most of those selected to the rank of admiral possess significant experience in DC. Without it, the future admiral would be of limited high-level value to the Navy. In hindsight, I recognize participating in the assignment process gave me a chance to influence my future viability.

The same applies in corporate and working for oneself. Sometimes you must step beyond what feels comfortable to invest in your future. These anecdotes of the assignments and processes are meant to highlight the value of cumulative experience. They also contributed directly to my reputation in the Navy and beyond.

* * *

During each phase of Jimmy Buffett's five-decade career, he continually pushed boundaries with new ventures. While his world-renowned music provided constant propulsion: that exploration into new opportunities required that he both learn from and work with others who could help. For example, Buffett's musical reputation gave him the cachet required to sing alongside Frank Sinatra—twice! He was also savvy enough to travel to a country music awards show with the intent of meeting new artists he could collaborate with. His initiative was rewarded with partnerships with Grammy winners such as George Strait and Kenny Chesney—and who hasn't heard "It's Five O' Clock Somewhere" with Alan Jackson?

I don't know if Jimmy Buffett purchased the *Ticonderoga* after the Key West trial after the race from Fort Lauderdale. I do know he has qualified as a private pilot and now owns multiple boats and aircraft of all types. He also continues to find innovative ways to deliver his music to fans, from building a live streaming empire to holding virtual events during the pandemic in 2020. His countless philanthropic endeavors also serve myriad causes, including manatee conservation, hurricane relief, oil spill relief and the group mentioned in the introduction, Freedom Fighter Outdoors. I'm not saying we can all be Jimmy Buffett, but his example illustrates how a growth mindset can create forward momentum in life that includes self-improvement and financial success and continually gives back to others.

* * *

My Navy career was beginning to peak in 2001 when I got a few lessons in humility. I was assigned to the Joint Operations Division (JOD) on the Joint Staff in the Pentagon. I had just left command of the USS *Laboon*, an Arleigh Burke destroyer, one of the Navy's most sophisticated platforms. The ship had done well because a highly trained crew came together at every opportunity.

Fresh off a successful deployment, I arrived for my first day at the Joint Staff and reported to the colonel in charge of the JOD, none other than Lloyd Austin. My first impression was that he was a redwood of a man—a physically imposing guy with a deep voice. While my driver's license may say I am 5'10," standing in front of Colonel Austin underscored that generous interpretation of the tape. He also had a reputation as a tremendous operator; at that point, he had been selected for one star. He would be a general soon but was awaiting his number for the promotion to take effect. However, he didn't use rank to convey credibility. His competent manner oozed credibility. He would later attain a four-star rank and eventually become secretary of defense. I was very interested to learn his approach to leadership and understand his expectations of me within this new team. In one of our first conversations, he made clear the importance of the work.

He looked me right in the eye and said, "You need to recognize that you're one layer removed from the trigger pullers out there." It was a little intense, but he had a surprisingly gentle interpersonal capacity. Then he went on to explain, "For the first six months, you're here to learn the ropes because you're in a different world now."

He wanted me to learn my position because he was an effective leader. Colonel Austin knew well that our role was to help interpret information from the combatant commanders so that the chairman of the Joint Chiefs of Staff and the secretary of defense could do their job in advising the president. Part of my job was to brief seniors, and he wanted me prepared for that responsibility. So, that day he sat me down and outlined my position. He told me I needed to know that the briefing materials I created could go to the president within a matter of hours from the time they left my printer.

This was next-level, top-of-one's-game stuff.

Compared to this level of intense scrutiny, command of a ship is incredibly cool. Captains of ships have a lot of autonomy. They have the authority to interpret their environment and make their ship perform within a given set of circumstances. The Joint Staff and this level of national security performance were miles removed from the responsibility and discretion for the operating in the fleet I had known. Colonel Austin wanted me to appreciate the difference at the outset.

He said, "You're on the spot for your piece of it, but for the first six months, you're not going to see any of those people."

The people to which Colonel Austin referred were the most senior civilians in government. I was now exposed for the first time to the level of leadership where civilian oversight of the military really takes place. Cabinet- and subcabinet-level officials and appointees would be the first consumers of our Joint Staff work. Pressures of the political environment, personal ambition and the clock all conspire to reduce the tolerance for errors to zero. Colonel Austin knew that errors, whether innocent or not, kill promising military careers. He took the time and provided appropriate top cover to allow my team of highly skilled leaders to grow into their new Joint Staff positions. I had learned along the way that some leaders deal better with pressure than others. In the military, we learn how to apply our training and skills to reduce or eliminate the negative aspects of pressure.

Colonel Austin did not learn these skills in a vacuum. I'm grateful to have served on a Joint Staff replete with the best of each service. I can name dozens from my time who went on to even greater levels of leadership within their service. Lieutenant General Greg Newbold, USMC, led the J-3, of which JOD was a part at the time. Leadership like I'm describing flows from the top and builds as it spreads across an organization.

That was a moment in my career that made me stand back. It was a powerful example of effective high-level leadership. Colonel Austin was protecting his team from a senior civilian who would see if a mistake was made and nearly universally react negatively. These people were used to commanding and interacting at the White House level. He was offering me a chance to adapt to the Washington apparatus. In that environment, you can get run over by the freight train if you don't understand what you're going up against.

I was impressed that he took the time to mentor in that way. It was an opportunity for personal growth and humility in action. At that level, why wouldn't you want to use your expertise in that capacity? At that point in my career, I thought I knew a lot, but that was a great lesson.

As an action officer in the Joint Staff, one of my roles was to secure approvals for various deployment orders. Combatant commanders routinely request various assets for specific purposes: aircraft carriers, submarines, vehicles, planes and troops. These assets are moved as the result of an approved deployment order. The action officers of J-3 were expected to walk deployment orders from one office to another to obtain signatures of the busy senior leaders.

When I arrived in J-3, I was provided a small, laminated card. It was a guide with all the room numbers of the key officials from whom we would regularly seek approvals.

It was an echo of the laminated light list of Captain Jim. A trusted method of keeping things straight! Underscoring the use of such a simple tool was the need to work quickly and accurately in what can be a high-pressure environment. It was a grinding tour that tests limits and reinforces how resilient we can be when tested.

My understanding of top-tier leadership continued to advance when I worked under Vice Admiral Cutler Dawson while I was a liaison of the Navy to Congress. He's a very smart guy, a leader who knows how to connect and support people to create influence. He made an effort to acknowledge my contributions and encourage me to grow. That was his style. For example, early in my time with him, he and I attended a meeting designed to prepare the secretary of the Navy to testify before Congress. It was a small meeting, only about six or eight people, and I realized too late that it was my job as the liaison to prepare the agenda and sample questions for the secretary. In a perfect world, my team would have checked with Hill contacts to see what issues were likely to arise during the hearing.

I was not prepared to facilitate that meeting, and everybody in the room knew it. I was filling in for a senior who had moved on, and I was too new to the role to appreciate my part. There were a few others in attendance who were eager to throw me under the bus to keep the heat off them, but Dawson took over. It was not his first congressional hearing, and it wasn't his first such prep meeting, but he understood it was mine. He led a productive discussion of the key points the secretary should give some extra thought. The bottom line was Admiral Dawson knew how to maintain SA and navigate the situation to accomplish our goals. He recognized the value in demonstrating how to properly execute the mission rather than calling out my shortcomings. Once again, a respected senior provided appropriate top cover that allowed me time to learn.

In another memorable meeting I attended with Dawson, I had been asked in advance to stay behind and discuss an issue with Admiral Mike Mullen, then serving as vice chief of naval operations. I was prepared and knew how and what I would say when I had my moment. I thought it was a good recommendation, or I would not have offered my input. I suggested a particular line of messaging to Congress about a program important to the Navy and about which I had very deep understanding.

Admiral Mullen listened intently but then quickly shut me down: "No. We're not going to do that." The meeting was over in about two minutes. I was really surprised that what made perfect sense at my level was so soundly rejected. It was a mildly deflating exchange.

As Admiral Dawson and I walked back to our offices, he casually threw an arm around my shoulders and said, "Sometimes it goes that way, Gene." I shook my head.

It was a simple gesture, but it meant a lot. There's no pleasure observing that the troubled program presents a perpetual messaging challenge with Congress to this day. I didn't have the same perspective as Admiral Mullen. It was also a lesson for me in knowing how to accept redirection and move on to the next issue.

Dawson's kind words and my growth mindset had value, and I later had several positive meetings with Admiral Mullen. As the Navy's Senate liaison, I would escort him to various meetings and facilitate introductions. When I was in a role to provide suggestions or recommendations about interactions with Congress, he always listened intently, asked tough questions and synthesized inputs with his other sources and indicators.

Corporate and military life both have limitations. As you come up through the military, there is a board selection process. It's transparent, and there's a schedule. Before a selection board, your official record is groomed, assuring day-for-day continuity of evaluations, as well as an up-to-date photo proving that you remain fit and trim. While board deliberations are secret, the fact that a board is scheduled is public knowledge, as is the individual being evaluated.

In a corporate setting, such boards don't exist. The

strategic plan of a company is not always common knowledge, and the myriad issues under consideration at any one time are often discussed in less visible channels. Succession planning may appear more official at the very top of the corporate ladder, but most transitioning military are not at that level of the corporate atmosphere. I observe that former military members are not often selected for corporate positions that are responsible for profit and loss. This is puzzling as the accountabilities of command are far more intense than profit and loss, but that's generally not how the business world views it. You might find out that a senior manager was selected for a promotion or new responsibility because the bosses discussed it during a game of golf over the weekend. It is difficult to maintain situational awareness when your knowledge of the environment is imperfect.

Your military career is public, and the waterfront knows if something happened—good and bad. You wear ribbons and pins that say where you've been and what you've done. We wear our career insignia with pride. If you don't promote up—it's up or out. It's not like you can go next door to the other US Navy. But in corporate, you can be promoted out of someone's world. Or you can be given a nice departure package and move from DC to Dallas and reinvent yourself within an industry. The story you tell is your story. In the military, that's not the case. Your accomplishments, your challenges, any problems are generally known—that's a big difference between the two worlds.

As my career advanced, I built the habit of identifying my position, evaluating my expertise and recognizing my personal and organizational limitations. By building these skills, I have been able to frame and reframe my experience to fit current goals and the opportunities at hand. I continue to refine and hone these skills as I advise new clients. The scenarios, variables, challenges and opportunities all build upon a broad base of experience.

These are learnable skills that you can apply to your situation as well. Experience builds confidence. Knowing your areas of expertise, your limitations and your position are important to be able to make successful moves in life.

6

BUILD A GREAT REPUTATION

"Be somebody people like to work with." -GM

Your peers promote you.

My dad gave me this sage advice as I prepared to leave for the Navy. At that time, I understood the concept of being a good crewmember. I learned about cooperation and coordination in high-stakes situations from my experience on Captain Jim's crew. When preparing to go to my first ship, I learned about teamwork from the perspective of the Navy. I found I could thrive in an atmosphere of healthy competition. I often heard the phrase, "cooperate to graduate," which means you work hard to inspire one another. You compete up to a point, but it's not about keeping someone else down. Everyone can be lifted in an environment of positive leadership.

I took this to the next level when the Navy gave me

the opportunity to get my master's in Monterey— another vote of confidence from my peers. Business calculus had to be conquered, as did variations on advanced accounting. The Navy made an investment in my future based on my early shipboard reputation. Classmates inspired me with healthy competition and helped me at the Naval Postgraduate School. This continued as I received support along the way from great guys like Taylor Skardon.

Each time I found a position where I could learn and thrive, I built my reputation and developed a new point of reference on my light list.

You can never hide from your reputation. You might be able to retell your story, but that's not the same thing. Your reputation is what people say about you when you're not around. If you have a great reputation, it opens the doors to opportunities. In the Navy, there is code for how one is described. There is a huge difference between a "good guy" and a "great guy." (Guy is not gender-specific in this case.) Shipmate can mean either—good or great. It's all in the inflection with which it's used: "airman" and "marine," for instance, can be used with either a derogatory or uplifting tone. If your shipmates think of you as a "great guy" and find themselves in a position to help you, they certainly will. Notice I referred to Taylor as a "great guy."

Finding new opportunities is natural when you are growing at a rapid rate. But how do you maintain a great reputation when you lack experience? By being humble.

Be somebody people like to work with. When my dad said my peers would promote me, it was just a different way to say don't be greedy, don't be selfish, don't be a jerk. These things go together.

The concept of your peers promoting you applies everywhere. It becomes a self-fulfilling sequence if you build a great reputation for being able to work effectively with others, recognize opportunities, act on those and get the job done. Through humility, you can add value to any situation. And it is a surefire way to build a great reputation along the way.

* * *

My Uncle Jack also believed in your peers promoting you.

As he built a career at John Hancock, Uncle Jack recognized that the training he received in the military helped him advance. He likened running a ship in the Navy to running a large organization, and he built on the experience he gained in the Navy. After 15 years at John Hancock, the company gave him the opportunity to attend Harvard Business School. This offered him new skills that he applied as he helped guide the organization through several major transitions in the early 1980s.

He said there were two ways to advance in business: to climb or get pushed. He considered himself fortunate to have been pushed to succeed by the people around him. He believed his strength came from his ability to build relationships with people who knew more than him about certain aspects of the business. He humbly believed that building relationships was the best way to advance.

The same has been true for me.

Uncle Jack's business relationships scored him an invitation to attend the 1987 America's Cup competition in Australia. The America's Cup, held every four years, is the oldest and most prestigious international yacht racing competition. An Australian yacht won the cup in the 1983 race, which was the first time in the history of the race that the Americans lost the cup. This set the scene for the hotly anticipated 1987 competition—a major event in the sailing world.

My dad called me in Monterey, where I was attending the Navy Postgraduate School. Julie had just given birth to Andrea, and I was focused on my studies, building my family and career. His excitement was palpable over the phone, even from thousands of miles away.

"I'm going to Australia with Jack for the America's Cup," my dad exclaimed.

As a sailing enthusiast, I followed the competition. Particularly that year because the American teams were all vying to regain the cup. I remember watching Walter Cronkite and Gary Jobson (who had long left the Naval Academy) reporting on the race from our house in California, knowing my dad and Uncle Jack were on that water somewhere. The races were thrilling, with an

American team triumphantly regaining the cup after some tense moments in the semifinals. Cronkite was at his peak, and he had a reputation as a sailing enthusiast; his presence reporting on the event brought significant mainstream media attention. Gary Jobson was commentating on sailing on ESPN, for which he would win a Cable Excellence Award. As I watched, I imagined the thrills Uncle Jack and my dad were experiencing, sharing the water with the best racing yachts in the world.

When he returned, my dad gave me a full account of his adventure. He described a week of meeting new people and exploring different boats and the waters off the coast of Western Australia. Excited about opportunities he had to make new friends from all over the world, he talked about spending time with some leaders in his industry from Japan. We discussed how he planned to stay in touch with these international business contacts who shared his enthusiasm for sailing.

"I'm sending everyone a copy of Jimmy Buffett's "Last Mango in Paris" cassette," my dad announced over the phone to me a few weeks after he returned from the trip.

He explained that Jimmy Buffett's music had been everywhere during the America's Cup events. Buffett was a mainstream success in the US at that point, but some of the international travelers my dad met on the trip were exposed to him for the first time. He thought a

Jimmy Buffett cassette was a great "thank you" present to send all his new contacts.

"Did they like Jimmy Buffett?" I asked after he explained.

He replied cheerfully, "Everyone likes Jimmy Buffett, Gene."

* * *

Finding success has a lot to do with believing the potential others see in you that you might not even see in yourself. They may not be able to bring that possibility to the surface, but if they believe in you, they become your advocates. Those relationships can lead to opportunities—based on your reputation. That's a strong case for building relationships and a solid reputation. It's great to be doing well, but people must know that you're doing well. Are you blowing your own horn? Is someone else blowing your horn? Is the Jimmy Buffett music even playing?

Humility has its place; however, we live in a world that demands a little marketing.

Reputation has different meanings in the civilian world. In corporate, there is a structure but not like the military. Your ability to advance is not always clearly defined or based on merit or your experience. There are many other forces at work. You can't always have a front-row seat to the golf course politics or five-year strategic plan of a corporation. In the corporate world, you can't even depend on a job title to indicate someone's relative importance in the big picture. Often, titles like manager or VP are awarded in a somewhat ceremonial capacity, although they do not indicate a higher level of experience or pay.

There are people you can let go of if they are no longer a positive participant in your success or a positive influence in your life. I have served and worked with many people over the years, and I can only remember a fraction of them by name and characteristics. I remain in contact with a select few. They really applied themselves and were superstars. You can't mentor everyone, and not everyone is the right mentor for you. Being selective in your relationships can be liberating. I value my relationships, but I don't feel the need to send a Christmas card to everyone I ever worked with or served with. This gives me the space to focus on what matters.

Your military relationships are lasting, but they don't require daily attendance. Shared history and commitment to the higher purpose and core values of service give us an unbreakable bond. I received a reminder of the difference between the contacts I made in the military in relation to the one I have from my time in the corporate world as I confirmed the stories in this book. I reached out to several story subjects. In every case, the response was immediate, friendly and constructive. That's not always the case within a corporation.

The fact is, corporations are always changing. They simply have to adapt quickly, and that means the workforce must adapt as well. The nature of corporate relationships can change as quickly and quietly as people change positions. Military people, who are accustomed to a different level of connection, can miss this dynamic unfolding right in front of them. Here's a simple test. If you returned to a unit in which you previously served twenty years ago, you would likely know the lay of the land, who's in charge and how they do what they do. If you walk into an office building to meet with Salesforce or Microsoft, for example, none of those lines will be as clear. Further, many in the building won't be able to outline it for you because they aren't 100 percent sure.

* * *

A lot of people end up clinging to their past, holding too tight to previous successful experiences. Long-term success depends on your ability to adapt.

This was a motivation when I started a PhD program at age 57. After writing my first book, I gained a greater appreciation of my talents gained through unique experiences. I learned that PhDs are about identifying gaps in existing knowledge and conducting research to fill the gap, thereby creating new knowledge. My experiences working with the federal funding process as a military operator, military budget expert, congressional fellow, corporate lobbyist and now trusted corporate advisor provide me a truly unique perspective on our government.

Filling a gap in knowledge requires a research plan, a scholarly approach and peer-reviewed validation. These are all symbols of the reputability of my studies. The degree will be something tangible I can look back on with pride. But it's also meant to be emblematic of the work I am doing. I'm still building my reputation. Why should a company stake its future on me if I'm not willing to do the same on myself?

In military service, it is customary to receive a ribbon or award at the end of each tour. These are symbolic of a mission accomplished and a job well done. Those end-of-tour ribbons carry a sense of completion, success and deep satisfaction at having honored a commitment to your coworkers and country. In the corporate world, they just give you cash—actually, it's not even cash; it's a direct deposit or a stock opportunity. Financial incentives are nice, but they are not a substitute for feeling like a key part of a successful mission with a higher purpose.

After several years of building my consulting business, I received three awards in my industry in 2020. I was named a Top Lobbyist by the National Institute for Lobbying and Ethics and received the Corrie Shanahan Memorial Award for Advanced Consulting. My firm was also identified as a 2020 Top Lobbying Firm by Bloomberg Government—one of the few solo practitioners to make the list. In 2021, I was inducted into the

Million Dollar Consulting Hall of Fame®, something I did not even know existed while I was in a corporate role. I was grateful for the feeling of recognition again, but more importantly, these were awards from my peers in the consulting community. Their acknowledgment was a signal that the moves I have made in professional development and personal growth are paying off.

7

LEARN MORE ABOUT LEADERSHIP

"Culture won't improve with time; it takes actions to change culture—yours or someone else's." -GM

A leader can impact everything through their tone of command. Throughout my military career, corporate years and life as a consultant, I have experienced many different types of leadership. In each role, I gathered valuable insights and lessons that have become my own leadership tools.

In the Navy, I thought I was a good leader because I could make a lot of quick decisions. I knew how to motivate and include everyone, and I knew when a change needed to be made for the good of the team. I have learned that I was really good at positional leadership, which has an underpinning in a hierarchy. Most military leaders (and followers) understand positional leadership well and know how to extract its maximum value.

What I didn't appreciate so much on active duty but that has flourished in my postmilitary career is the gift of my ability to influence. That ability to influence is something that many people have and don't know, especially in the military. With each assignment, each deployment, each operation, you are meeting different personalities, learning new ways to communicate, becoming more flexible and adding tools to your toolbox. Eventually, you can recognize how to use that knowledge and the ability to convey information to influence outcomes.

In the corporate world, you must sometimes use your influence to convince people that you have knowledge. That role of influence is still a strong one. The ability to influence is an important part of a business leader's value. A leader knows not only how to convey quality information that affects the outcomes but clearly explains to superiors why it should matter. When you are being challenged to produce better outcomes, you need to draw from all your experiences and help people open their minds to new possibilities. Business continually demands new thinking.

A lot of bosses can't wait to be the first one to speak or hog the airtime. Leadership can be demonstrated in how you stand up for your points of view without waiting for the boss's opinion. In my consulting role, I worked with a small family-owned company, and the president was a bit of a big dog. In a meeting, he made a declarative statement in the face of facts to the contrary, and I took him on. And it was fascinating to watch the group dynamic shift in that meeting—to watch people roll. None of his own team stood up to him. They didn't want to be on the boss's bad side, but the ability to command respect requires you to know your stuff. Sometimes it's not easy knowing you're right.

Having the self-assuredness to correct someone who is wrong can be done tactfully and in a way that's not combative. That's how we grow.

In consulting, I'm not paid to be deferential. Deference pervades the military and all hierarchical organizations that rely on positional leadership. It's a completely human tendency to defer to one's senior. In guiding clients to new positions, deference wastes time. Influence using one's credibility and knowledge carries the day.

In my leadership training, I encountered a concept that perfectly captures what can happen when business leaders stop advancing. It's called "executive derailment" or sometimes "career derailment." When a previously successful leader stops being able to do their job effectively, it's considered derailment. There are many factors that can contribute to this, like personal struggles outside the workplace and failure to accept changing corporate culture.

A derailed executive is toxic to the company culture. They might deliver big sales, but people struggle to work with them, and it can be tolerated but only for so long—then there is a tipping point. Maybe they have a long track record of success but now seem to be struggling to adapt, deliver results or communicate effectively. In the executive coaching world, this person is called a "derailing executive."

In the Navy, this person can be a captain or even a chief petty officer.

I'm not making light of this issue, but there was a time in my Navy service when it wasn't unusual to have a "screamer" as a captain. For some, it seems to be routine to bully and be abrasive. But like with any bully, it's insecurity that brings out that behavior. I'm happy to report that for decades there has been a cultural shift in the Navy away from this negative leadership style, and it's now quite rare in all branches of the military. It was a big change for the better when those behaviors were no longer tolerated.

Not only is this style of leadership now recognized as toxic and ineffective, but the culture of the service had to keep pace with technology. Today, anyone can just break out a cell phone and suddenly your tirade is going viral. I think back to some early moments in my career and, if there had been cell phones, that information flow would certainly have changed the behaviors of some of my superiors.

In the military, those negative behaviors are largely contained or suppressed. There are levels of punishment in the military that can't be used in corporations. After experiencing many leadership styles in the Navy, I now recognize that the screaming executive is compensating for insecurity. The CEO that is calm, controlled and thoughtful presents a more overtly effective exterior. They're more trustworthy. That's not to say that you can't lose your temper occasionally and still be professional—but not routinely.

After a couple of tours, I learned I would never get two bosses in a row of any kind. This was good news and bad news. You would have a great captain or leader, but you typically would not get two in a row. Likewise, you knew that the clock was ticking on any toxic leader. The Navy was grappling with its own methods of leadership and how it was taught and developed at all levels.

The infamous Tailhook convention in 1991 and subsequent controversy proved critical to improving military culture. The convention gathered members of several branches of the military in Las Vegas. Throughout the weekend, the event was the scene of very excessive public alcohol consumption, improper and indecent conduct and actions that led to allegations of nearly 100 sexual assaults on both men and women. There was a civilian outcry over the military's lack of prosecution of the alleged sexual assaults. While this was a horrific event, it prompted a seismic shift in the culture. The improvements in military leadership training in the last 30 years have been significant and have largely created a positive impact across the armed forces.

* * *

The military has core values that remain unwavering as you move from command to command. You learn to embody concepts of honor, courage, commitment and duty. You serve your country, ship, shipmate and self. The values became so ingrained that every military person brings with them into a situation. This intrinsic connection to the mission is part of what makes those who retire from the military so uniquely qualified to be leaders. When you lose touch with the core values of your organization, it's a red flag that you need to move on.

One of my favorite memories of a senior officer embodying the core values of the Navy happened while I was in Flag Officer detailing in 1996. After the birth of our fourth child, Rachel, my wife brought all the kids to visit me at my office near the Pentagon. We had an admiral visiting at the time, Steve Abbott, who went on to become a four-star and then serve as deputy commander-in-chief of the US European Command. Julie was making her way into the office, juggling a stroller with our new baby and three other kids. I was behind my desk and too slow to get up and over to the door.

This admiral was all over it, like the mayor of a small town, conveying warmth and welcome for the Navy family members walking through the door. That was a one-off interaction, but his utter humility really struck me. He was a busy man, there to talk about important matters with my boss, yet in a heartbeat, he shifted to the highest priority in the room. Was it honor, courage and commitment? I say yes because it was all wrapped up in decency and humility. We should all know how to recognize those moments.

* * *

When I served on the Joint Staff, my initial assignment was as the Navy person in the Joint Operations Division (JOD). I was placed in that position because I had experience leading ships equipped with Tomahawk missiles —the US foreign policy tool of choice throughout the 1990s. At that point in my career, I understood how to bloom where I was planted. I was eventually moved into the front office and served as the executive assistant to the two-star US Army general who would later wear four stars. From there, I was soon assigned to serve as the assistant to the three-star marine, Lieutenant General Greg Newbold.

That was my world on the morning of September 11, 2001. I was sitting at my desk in the JOD, which is located on the eastern side of the Pentagon building. As usual, the morning news was on, and my workmates and I were drinking coffee discussing the issues of the day. Then reports began that the World Trade Center had been struck by a plane. Video came on the news immediately.

I remember watching the smoke billowing from the

building and commenting, "How does a small plane just fly into a building in New York City?"

My desk mate, an F-16 pilot, replied, "That's no small plane—that's a commercial airliner."

As we sat, struggling to make sense of what we were seeing on TV, we heard a distant rumble. My chair shifted on its own, just slightly. Seconds later, the sound of shrieking alarms filled the halls of the Pentagon.

Something was very wrong.

Word came that the building had been struck by a plane and that we must evacuate. My mind was racing. I distinctly remember marveling that the Pentagon building is so massive that one side was experiencing the sheer terror and destruction of the plane crash while my chair barely moved.

Fire drills are routine at the Pentagon, so the evacuation was an orderly departure—at least on my side of the building. We evacuated to the River Entrance. Immediately people were attempting to share personal cell phones to contact families. Not everyone had a personal cell phone in 2001, and some had left phones at their desks, believing we would go back inside shortly. But this was not a drill.

Cell phones proved useless, as networks crashed across the country.

Soon, Air Force jets could be seen overhead. Helicopters began landing on the River Entrance lawn since the traditional Pentagon helipad was obscured by the crash. The helicopters were there to evacuate key personnel to a remote watch site. Plans of which I had no specific knowledge were unfolding right in front of me. I stood there thinking, at some point, key decision-makers had laid plans for mass casualties and evacuations at the Pentagon. I was part of plans laid for something we could not fully plan. That is the essence of military thinking.

Shortly thereafter, JOD members were instructed to return to the building and fall in with the command center watch team. We didn't yet know what the military response to the events of the day would be, but an organization quickly assembled to figure it out.

It was late that evening by the time I finally got to connect with Julie by phone on the watch floor. Like so many families that day, she and our daughters had spent the entire day fearing the worst. They had no way of knowing my great fortune being on the opposite side of the Pentagon from the crash. As we know now, it was a defining day for the country, with nearly 3,000 people losing their lives and close to 6,000 others injured. Friends and colleagues were lost, but many heroes emerged.

It was full dark by the time I could go home. As I opened the outside door to walk toward my car in the Pentagon's south parking lot, I could smell the smoldering fire. Smoke was still lingering, rising from the other side of the massive building where I spent the last 12 hours. It would be months before I could process what had just happened. I later learned that 55 military members perished in the Pentagon that day and never had the opportunity to process, to count their blessings or to contemplate their future contributions in this life.

After September 11, 2001, everything changed. The priorities of the government response quickly shifted from Afghanistan, where we knew the terrorists were primarily organizing and hiding, to Iraq. The focus in the Middle East became weapons of mass destruction.

The case for the war with Iraq was weak, and it was politically motivated. General Greg Newbold, the three-star marine I supported as an executive assistant at the time, resigned because he did not support the way the US went to war with Iraq. The US was going it alone without broad international support. We did not have a coalition; the world was not with us as had been the case in other major efforts.

I observed General Newbold closely and admired that he took such a principled stand without making a big scene. He didn't make a public challenge or disparage the civilian leaders or his Marine Corps—but he had to act because the war went against his values. It was a powerful example of senior leadership and staying true to their ideals. This type of leadership is exceptionally uncommon and calls on one's personal strength of the highest order.

During the first year of the Iraq war, I recall hearing an interview on NPR. The ignorant guest prognosticated that a war with Iraq could cost the US "as much as $1 billion." This was a gross underestimation. Direct costs alone are known to have cost one trillion dollars—a factor of 1,000 times higher. Adding indirect costs, the number approaches two trillion dollars. Not to mention the loss of life.

I subsequently participated in multiple aspects of our war in Iraq and recall regularly thinking it would ultimately be deemed a strategic blunder to shift from Afghanistan to Iraq as we did. The decisions of taking a nation to war are made by elected civilians and their confirmed team. The military advises but salutes the decision either way once it has been made. Leadership of our military and our nation is highly complex and not easily distilled into media soundbites. Yet we consume our information in soundbites.

Being a good leader and supporting strong leadership are far easier to do than being bad at either. Poor leaders are often ill-prepared for their role and project that discomfort onto others. While you can learn from an example of what not to do, it's no fun for anyone. Who doesn't want to be part of a winning team?

It takes strong leadership to see beyond failure. To dust off and move on to the next thing.

* * *

In 1990 I was junior lieutenant on the USS *Nicholson* when I faced one of my most difficult leadership roles. After being in the position for all of two days, I distinctly remember realizing I was less well prepared than I might have hoped. That while I had been getting my master's in Monterey for two years, those lessons did not directly apply to leadership aboard a ship. My single early tour of one ship might prove detrimental. I wasn't falling in on a strong organization, and I didn't yet have a plan figured out.

In a moment of discouragement, I thought to myself, "How am I even going to survive this tour?"

The tour started on the wrong foot and never really got back on track. I arrived during what's called a 3M inspection. It tests how well a ship documents its maintenance activities. As the operations officer, I was not responsible for a lot of equipment. It should have been a cakewalk. For example, sailors in my department had to do a daily test on the radar screen, not complicated tasks like with engineering, high voltages and tagout procedures. And still my department failed their portion of the inspection. It's almost unheard of for an operations department to fail at 3M. I wondered if I could figure it out.

It wasn't long after that, the ship failed its major engineering operation. It's called an operational propulsion plant examination (OPPE). I wasn't specifically responsible, but everyone helps the engineer. There are aspects of OPPE that require the entire ship to participate. The ship failed the examination miserably for all kinds of reasons. It was a difficult time on the ship. We were the losing team, and everyone knew it.

That is until the engineer was replaced with LT

Taylor Skardon, who later selflessly recommended me for the plum position he was being offered. He came on board and made a tremendous difference in how the ship operated. His approach was by the book, but LT Skardon was extremely personable and was just the special tonic the leadership team needed. We did a six-month deployment and then retook the engineering inspection: the ship passed with flying colors. The transformation of the ship was dramatic.

Taylor Skardon was the positive force behind that ship's turnabout.

More than a decade later, when I was in command for the first time, I recognized that maintaining a ship's good reputation is almost as difficult as building it. When I took command of the USS *Laboon* in 1999, I was working for phenomenal leaders, taking over a great ship and riding high on a promotion that put me in command several years ahead of the career trajectory I had anticipated. Shortly after I took command, the ship faced a congressionally required comprehensive inspection called an INSURV, an examination of every department of a ship.

Ordinarily, a commander might have months to prepare for such an inspection, but ours was to be a short-notice INSURV—the Navy command equivalent of a pop quiz. Thanks to the solid infrastructure and great leaders, the ship passed the test with flying colors. I had inherited a great ship led by Commander Mike Mahon, who would later become a rear admiral before moving into industry. Mike ran a great ship, and the INSURV success proved an ingrained positive culture of readiness. The "like new" standard was alive in *Laboon*.

Laboon was subsequently selected to escort the aircraft carrier USS *Eisenhower* to the Adriatic Sea in a 30-knot sprint, leaving the rest of the battle group to proceed at the traditional 15-knot transit speed. World events had necessitated the carrier's earlier-than-planned arrival. Rather than 10 days, we sprinted in just under six days, requiring *Laboon* to travel at top speed in front of the carrier the entire time. Maintaining a safe distance in front of an aircraft carrier at a consistent speed of 30 knots for that extended period tested all our systems aboard the ship. Any material issue with the performance of the engineering plant would have meant us making less than 30 knots, and the nuclear-powered carrier would then outpace its escort and leave us behind. That would have been both embarrassing and not operationally sound. Once again, we passed this real-life test with flying colors.

Although it can be tempting to take full credit for this type of triumph, I know that the integration of systems and crew that makes a ship successful doesn't happen overnight. In *Laboon*, I inherited a great ship, and my adaptation of the team helped make it even better. This early command experience stuck with me when I was assigned to the USS *Philippine Sea* in 2005 and 2006. Shortly after taking command, I learned we would deploy in an out-of-cycle deployment, and I would lead two other ships to the Arabian Gulf. That meant within six weeks, we were going to deploy.

We were having some engineering difficulties, and I made the tough decision to let the engineer go to his next assignment ashore early. His operational rise was over, and it was time to make the change. I knew from my previous experiences a new team would be vital. I let him go early and knowingly took a gap of his billet to let someone else float up to the job in the interim until the arrival of a scheduled replacement. The someone from within was a limited duty officer, an engineering specialist who was ready to lead. He had earned his spurs the hard way coming up in the Navy. This was his moment. I had complete faith in his technical and leadership skills.

During our transit through the Suez Canal, my trust in him clouded my judgment. Some brief background on Suez Canal transits. Ships run single file, north or south, in a highly orchestrated parade of ships. Egyptian ship pilots embark for the ride. My experience with the pilots was never noteworthy. I appreciate that some are quite good; they didn't seem to find their way to my ships any of the six times I made the transit. US warships always lead the parade north or south. We pay a premium for that position in line with the idea that a US warship will never get stuck in the canal behind another ship with a problem.

In 2021 the incident involving the commercial container ship *Ever Given* proved the value of that thinking. When the 1,300-foot cargo ship, owned by a large Japanese corporation and weighing 220,000 tons, ran aground in the canal, it caused an international incident. The event triggered a traffic jam of hundreds of boats stuck in the canal and interrupted global supply chains. It took six days to free the ship and allow traffic to begin moving through the canal again. While the causes, liabilities and financial impacts remain unknown, the incident has prompted innovations in new safety measures, pilot training protocols and boat designs.

The scene of this incident is roughly halfway through the Suez Canal in an area called Bitter Lake. This is where either the northbound or southbound convoy waits briefly for the other convoy to pass. While I was in command of the USS *Philippine Sea*, we were temporarily anchored in Bitter Lake. The interim engineer asked for permission to lock a shaft for a brief maintenance event. I agreed, knowing we could unlock it quickly.

About 20 minutes later, the temporary pilot barked, "Captain, we must go now!" Suddenly we're late, and ships were moving into their single-line formation—the line we were supposed to lead. We retrieved the anchor, and I ordered the shaft to be unlocked. We began to proceed on one shaft to our lead position in the convoy.

The engineer called up and said, "I can't get it unlocked—we need to come to all stop to do so."

That was not an option at this point. Ships were

lining up, and we were now entering the lower portion of the canal at slow speed. Looking out over the bridge wing, the boulders and rocks that line the entrance to the canal are clearly visible and a reminder of how precarious the transit can be if something were to fail.

I figured the worst-case scenario would be that we proceed with one shaft locked.

Here's the problem. My mind was recalling the speed limits for a destroyer with a locked shaft. A cruiser's limits are not the same. This meant we would have to maintain a limited speed during the last stretch of the southbound canal trip. I admitted my error to the interim engineer and the officer of the deck. We agreed we'd do the best we could to get through the last few hours of the transit and come to a stop when we were free to maneuver in the Red Sea. My position as captain and assumption by all around me that I was correct reflects a serious flaw of positional leadership and something my crew and I would subsequently address.

The pilot kept checking his calculations and strongly encouraged me to proceed at a specific speed. I insisted that I was doing just that. The engineering team and bridge team understood we were actually going as fast as we could on a locked shaft without causing damage to the other engine and propulsion system.

Upon clearing the canal, I radioed the two US ships transiting behind me to inform them that I needed to come to all stop for a few minutes to unlock a shaft. I instructed them to proceed ahead and told them we would catch up. Of course, they did just that, following an order and moving on smartly. This marked the end of an exhausting day. I was responsible and would have been accountable had anything gone wrong.

I had violated established procedure for locking a shaft. It's not something that should ever be done on the fly except in an emergency. My trusting relationship with the interim engineer had clouded my judgment. The consequences could have been something far more serious. It was an important reminder upon entering a new theater of operations. There's a reason the rules and procedures exist. They save equipment and save lives. We all rallied around that lesson on board.

Another valuable lesson I learned during that deployment was the power of a team of strong teams. In command of USS *Philippine Sea*, I had the opportunity to serve under a British one-star admiral, technically referred to as a commodore in the Royal Navy. The three-ship "task group" I was leading would arrive out of cycle to support antipiracy operations. We were a bonus of three US ships added to his multinational charge. During this assignment, we were given quite a bit of autonomy to create and implement plans to detect and deter the ubiquitous piracy problem that was not abating. I found it exhilarating. Commodore Tony Rix was an exceptional leader who encouraged creativity and fostered it throughout his organization. His perspective helped me grow and even better understand the value of a strong team with diverse opinions and methods. Working with him made me realize there were lots of good ways to get the job done.

After that successful deployment, USS *Philippine Sea* faced a regularly scheduled INSURV. The ship was a 17-year-old cruiser, which presented the challenges of equipment maintenance on an older vessel. Part of the test is operating the ship at full power. That doesn't just mean running with all engines online. It means producing measurable power from the engineering plant that will propel the ship at top speed. Myriad details are associated with this effort, including training and maintenance documentation, calibration and fuel management, among others. Typically, during a full-power demonstration, the ship increases speed incrementally from zero to top end.

It's a specific test and a culminating point of an in-port phase followed by the underway portion of the inspection. The ship had faced down the many challenges of INSURV leading up to this moment, and we were ready. We were underway, operating near Jacksonville, Florida, on a beautifully crisp day. Gas turbine engines love low humidity conditions, and I knew we were beginning a good run. Feeling confident on the way out to deep water, I ordered the ship to increase speed, 15 knots, 20 knots, 25 knots, Flank 3. The ship was just purring—exactly as it was supposed to. Satisfied we were ready for the full power run in a few hours, I ordered us to slow to five knots. No point burning excess fuel on the way out, I thought.

Bang!

As the ship went from doing above 30 knots to five knots, one of the four gas-turbine engines broke—a catastrophic failure of a metal part that didn't agree with my plan to change its temperature so quickly in the cool air.

"You have got to be kidding me," I said, along with a few other choice words.

That type of equipment failure is a showstopper. It meant we would not be doing a full-power run that day, as one of the four engines would now be unavailable until we could replace the failed part. To get through that inspection, we would ultimately have to borrow the critical part from another ship, which meant another ship consciously cannibalizing the part to lend to us until the new part would be flown in.

The waterfront is a small town; everyone knew we didn't perform as hoped despite a great effort.

The engineering inspector commented to me that it's widely known you can't go from over 30 knots to five knots in cool air. "The metal parts just can't take it."

It was a moment of defeat for me. This was my sixth gas turbine ship. The technology is extraordinarily durable, yet the part had broken. It really didn't matter why at this point. The engineering team was robbed of a clean victory in the full-power run because of a spontaneous decision I made.

The ability to have perseverance and resilience in tense moments is a unique skill developed in military life. Not everything goes to plan. It's the process of having a plan that allows you to deal with the unexpected. If you use the tools at your disposal, you can become a stronger leader.

* * *

There is no replacement for the totality of the command of a ship at sea. It was the ultimate leadership training, and I was privileged to command two ships. Now I have found a way to use what I have learned to train other leaders and guide aspiring leaders to new positions. I find it gratifying to help companies to do more than they thought they could by showing them a different way to view their challenges.

The impact is not just in dollars for the company. There are jobs and families those jobs support. Further, there's the national security impact of companies providing much-needed products and services. I marvel that I was once able to serve in and then lead the crews of warships valued at over $1 billion; now I am helping my clients' companies to earn billions for the good of the companies and the nation.

The sense of satisfaction I get from entrepreneurship is beyond anything I experienced while working for a corporation. My vision of consulting was narrow. I saw consultants as able to provide niche support for a missing piece in an organization. Really great consultants provide value beyond the immediate task. I try to understand the challenge a company president faces in its totality and can often share perspective, encouragement and occasionally direction: this helps them do even better.

In the corporate world, my title was VP, yet I had no direct reports. The company had many VPs of similar grade. I was reminded of my father sharing that VP titles are often dispensed like that at community banks, so customers always feel they are speaking with someone in authority. I understood authority well from my time in command. Authority is the power to make decisions inherent in your role. I observe that authority is generally not well distributed in many corporations. It's often watered down through either layers of leadership or the dreaded committee. When I became an SVP, it felt ceremonial. As someone who was used to an operational leadership position, I felt a void. The compensation was great; the sense of fulfillment was not. Many companies in transition through acquisition, organizational change or losing to competitors see their workforces struggling to maintain footing.

I took responsibility for things that were well beyond my job description, but I wanted to do more. I was personally struggling with the fact that there wouldn't be people to lead or more to do. My role had a clear ceiling, but the job did mean I could enjoy other aspects of life. In retrospect, it wasn't a great corporate experience for me because it wasn't a great fit. I observe many postmilitary people in corporate roles experiencing a similar phenomenon—the authority and accountability often don't align with the military leader's capabilities.

Ultimately, the decision to leave the corporate world was made for me. But it was the best decision. When my position was redefined and I was no longer part of that team, I finally had the perspective to recognize how unfulfilled I had been. And then I began to understand my lack of fulfillment was a failure to invest in myself.

It wasn't until I embraced my leadership capabilities when I went out on my own that I was able to further develop and flourish. But I recognize the difficulty of pursuing that gray area. It can be very intimidating to be your own boss after decades of structure. The self-editing and the fear that I see in others was present in me, but you can't see it when you're living it.

I use the word *fear* intentionally. Many stay put for far too long out of some sense of fear: fear of losing benefits, fear of finding suitable compensation, fear of being worthy enough to earn more in a different role, fear of finding a better role.

Learning high-level leadership requires flexibility and willingness to admit mistakes. True leaders embrace lifelong learning. I absorbed this lesson in the supportive structure of Navy leadership, surrounded by key mentors who encouraged me to grow. My supporting role of today is not something you will ever see on a billboard, but there is validation and fulfillment beyond words in the work. Every week I find myself synthesizing a career of highly unique experiences in ways that help companies prosper.

While my formative leadership experiences are specific to my own Navy service, I contend that any military member can comb their experiences and find similar significant points of learning. Those who serve in the US military are part of a community that places immense value and responsibility on effective leaders. Once you understand how to apply those lessons to life after military retirement, that level of exposure to leadership training will pay off exponentially.

8

PRACTICE DIPLOMACY

"What would Jimmy Buffett do?" -Alan Jackson

Diplomacy requires that we can negotiate complex structures and planning with flexibility and presence. Whether you're transitioning out of the military or changing roles in your career, understanding diplomacy makes you a strong leader.

Finding structure in the chaotic is a skill people develop in the military. Procedures help navigate problems in the absence of a clear understanding of solutions. Being able to negotiate a complex web of protocols without losing sight of the larger goal often separates good leaders from great ones. And it requires diplomacy.

Throughout my years in service, I not only learned about the importance of understanding organizational structure. I also developed a complex understanding of our legislative process. I have synthesized my experiences to create a product my clients need. I bring a deep understanding of the structure my clients need to get connected to government funding. Many see government sales through the lens of a proposal or contracting process, thereby missing a multitude of opportunities to help their company and help the government do better. I interpret that entire landscape for clients, lifting their sights to broader and longer-lasting opportunities.

My unique skillset is being able to think through to the future desired outcomes and connect those goals to required tasks. It's not a natural gift but one I have learned to recognize and use to my advantage. In my role as a consultant, connecting to funding is exactly what I do for my clients—but I must use diplomacy. They often don't understand the fundamental processes, and it's my job to educate them. If you haven't worked inside the government apparatus, it is very difficult to appreciate its intricacies.

Diplomacy is vital in situations where there is an element of risk. Military personnel learn how to mitigate risks, which is a valuable skillset to apply to a subsequent career. I am hired to advise and interact with company presidents and CEOs. They are paying me to tell them what their immediate subordinates might not be comfortable saying (or might not know). I must weigh the responsibilities and risks of my current role. The CEO or president could let me go if I can't make a connection with them. I'm working without a safety net, but I'm comfortable with that reality. Like in any military operation, I know how to set those concerns aside. It's about perspective. We're peers, in it together; I want them to do well.

Military people gain this perspective on active duty but can lose it when embedded in a corporate culture because the element of risk is missing. Decisions on active duty can mean injury, death or at least mission failure. Without those extreme consequences to motivate us, we can become skittish in our decision-making. After I stepped away from the corporate world, I recognized this.

Learning to apply the kind of diplomacy and decisive action required during military service has helped me thrive in business.

I served in a congressional fellowship in 2003 after the Joint Staff. I had been selected for captain, and this was another growth opportunity. Throughout government, mid- and senior-level personnel often perform fellowships in other agencies to exchange talent and understanding. As a fellow somewhat senior in rank, I was assigned to the office of then-Senator Thad Cochran, the ranking member and then chairman of Defense Appropriations.

I went into that situation with a growth mindset, thinking my priorities were to first build expertise and then establish relationships. I did not recognize at first how important my existing expertise was to those relationships. I thought for sure my role would require a level of diplomacy and understanding of the big picture. That was before I realized the congressional office organizational chart was flat. There is one healthcare person, one veterans' person, one agriculture person and so on. The committee members have so much on their plates, they rely on those around them to track and categorize volumes of information and give them the highlights. I quickly realized that a vital part of my job was being able to fill gaps in other peoples' understanding without bias. That required diplomacy.

Such strategic diplomacy was at work one day when I was to accompany Senator Cochran to a meeting with the chairman of the Joint Chiefs, General Myers. As we walked back from the Capitol to the office toward the meeting place, I was giving the senator the background on what would be discussed, and he turned to me and said, "Remind me again who General Myers is?"

As chairman of the Joint Chiefs, General Myers was the senior-most officer on the Joint Staff and the senior military advisor to the president. Senator Cochran had no understanding of the situation we were about to enter. I had just come out of the Joint Staff Operations directorate, so I was positioned to see the big picture and convey the crucial points to him.

It was an awakening for me. Until that point, I had never given much thought to legislative work after the

Navy. Serving in Washington allowed me to build my skills in diplomacy and recognize the value in my unique skillset. Recognizing that you know more than your superiors is one job, but being humble enough to appropriately navigate that responsibility is quite another.

As a senior member of the entire Appropriations Committee, Senator Cochran was not only responsible for funding defense but also in charge of funding the entire government. An enormous array of issues and responsibilities reside under that umbrella. I recognized in that moment that there was no way of knowing what's on people's plates. Being an effective advisor requires a keen awareness of knowledge gaps and the ability to fill them without drawing attention to yourself.

The elaborate procedures of the Pentagon were unknown to Senator Cochran. None of it exists on Capitol Hill in the same form. When I looked at the big picture, I recognized Senator Cochran had to maintain situational awareness from an entirely different perspective than me. The scope of his duties was far beyond anything I had ever experienced on a bridge watch, in command or on my boat.

Perspective matters. Applying your experience with an appreciation for your surroundings matters. That's diplomacy.

* * *

My exposure to high-level diplomacy continued when I ran the Navy's Senate office beginning in 2006. The time I spent as a Senate liaison allowed me to be around some truly extraordinary leaders. Up close and personal, politics aside, our nation has been blessed with some phenomenal leaders in Congress. The Navy Senate liaison office helps coordinate international travel for approved congressional delegations, known as CODELs.

In this role, I had the opportunity to travel with the late Senator Richard Lugar. Lugar was an absolute gentleman and scholar who constantly fed his intellect. His work ethic was as strong as his pursuit of knowledge. I spent days with him, alone and in small groups. His lifelong pursuit of helping rid the world of excessive nuclear and chemical biological weapons required a velvet touch. I was fortunate enough to accompany him on many trips to some very remote parts of the world in the exercise of his authority as chairman of the Senate Foreign Relations Committee.

For senators of real character, these were not just jobs they held—these were beliefs in how international affairs could be *and should* be. We were sent to some very remote places that I couldn't even point to on a map today without some help. In the case of Senator Lugar's trips, we would land in Moscow or Kazakhstan, for example, and then be driven a couple hours in one direction to tour nonproliferation sites. These are sites that we are allowed to tour and inspect to make sure the

world is complying with the international nonproliferation treaties, and they're allowed to do the same to us.
That is difficult and thankless work that these leaders do
for the greater good—not just of the US but the world as
well.

When you meet the people on the other side of the
US diplomatic equation, you see how much our service
on the world stage means to them. I have visited
numerous American Battlefield Monuments Cemeteries
in Italy, Belgium and France, among others. The people
of those countries cry to this day that Americans gave
their lives to save them. I've observed senators and
congresspeople calling the loved ones of those buried in
such cemeteries with tears in their eyes as they helped a
family member make a connection to that fallen soldier
and family member. The connection to history and to
my uncles who participated and were spared is real.

Unfortunately, the lasting impact of historical events
is not often part of our national discourse today. The
average American doesn't get to see the importance of
these diplomatic connections that span generations.
Those diplomatic relationships between nations had an
impact on me. It showed me how fragile global peace
can be.

I also traveled with the late Senator John McCain
quite a bit during the lead-up to the 2008 election. This
was a particular honor because he had served in my
exact job decades before. McCain was known for sharp
political positions. These were positions carefully

considered and based on his world experience and the support of a close team of advisors. I watched interactions with world leaders at the highest levels. I was in the room for nearly every meeting during our trips, not because I had a part but because the senator saw me as part of the team and knew it was important for me to learn. His astute instinct for leadership was an honor to witness firsthand.

McCain would rarely let his work ethic relax on a trip. If there was a short period of downtime, he couldn't just enjoy a cappuccino: he had to do something. We once had 90 minutes of unexpected dead time in Paris, so Senator McCain asked if we could go see Napoleon's tomb. Arrangements were made, and the car arrived to take us to the location, where we were immersed in this experience, a self-guided tour at Invalides. I wasn't that interested, but McCain was totally engrossed. He was completely immersed for 60 minutes, and then we raced to the next meeting. He packed every day as full as he could. The trips were exhausting for me, and he was three decades my senior. It was an interesting example of a person committed to diplomacy and lifelong learning.

Senator Joe Lieberman often accompanied McCain on many of these trips. Lieberman is a rockstar statesman in his own right. I believe his many accomplishments and positive influence on the international stage are not well-known enough. He is a tremendous conduit between Israel and the United States. He lives a life of devotion to his faith; some people have a hard time processing that level of commitment. I have seen him walk to the Senate on a snowy Saturday and witnessed him observing his faith on trips. His devotion to his work and faith are powerful. McCain and others in the CODELs understood and allowed appropriate space for it. I see Senator Lieberman living his higher purpose. To witness it up close left a powerful impression.

Former Senator Jon Kyl was also an impressive diplomat and leader I had a chance to accompany on international travel. I was sitting across from Kyl when he was charged with communicating the US position to Middle Eastern financiers and bankers. In those meetings, he made it clear their best option for those on the other side of an issue was to get on board. Kyl knew how to convey a message with words both spoken and unspoken. This made watching him work fascinating.

The congressional leaders that serve on the defense and intelligence committees often go to Paris, Munich and Frankfurt en route to remote assignments. We see footage of them at Heathrow, but no one catches them as they disembark in Azerbaijan! Most people don't understand the effort those members make to be informed and to see global issues for themselves.

People are entirely too dismissive of how hard the job is. It takes a lot of work, and some of them are older. McCain and Lugar were well into their 70s, for example. Some of the fact-finding involved in diplomatic work puts those members in front of people with questionable credibility. They are required to meet with the opposition leaders, and some of those "leaders" are a bit dubious in character.

I remember watching McCain sitting across from an Iraqi leader. The topic was black market oil. We all knew it was a reality—people were making money, yet they were sitting in front of us denying it. McCain knew, but he also understood that wasn't the place to call them out. We have intricate channels and methods of extracting truth. Diplomacy requires a highly attuned level of SA combined with humility, which translates to knowing when to act or remain still. Maintaining presence to interpret the room takes practice—and patience.

It's a gift to know when to simply observe.

I'm convinced people like Lugar, McCain, Lieberman and Kyl contributed to the long-standing global peace we have known since WWII. Senators of stature, regardless of party, represent the nation but also help interpret our national decisions for foreign leaders. In each case, I observed different highly effective styles of leadership and communication. In several instances, it was clear the world leader on the other side of the table was not being forthcoming. In each instance, I witnessed the senators, in their own ways, send signals that it was time for those world leaders to adjust.

We need more people like that—who can see the greater good and rise above themselves. They looked problems in the eye, recognized the risks and put themselves on the line. It didn't matter the politics; their positions had substance. Their characters were unshakable.

* * *

Success is dependent on how your personal systems and strategies are organized. We learn in service that process can help eliminate surprises or repeat failures. Learning to translate this skillset to life after the military can give former service members an advantage. First, however, you must adjust your processes to match your current situation. This transition requires an element of diplomacy and can take months, even years. But it is time well spent.

My dad once told me you could always pick the IBM person out of a crowd of executives at a trade show. Maybe it was the ubiquitous dark suit or the air of confidence that comes with working for the industry leader. Similarly, I believe you can pick out a military person in any environment. This is often because, on some level, their personal systems have carried over from service. The fitness level, the attention to personal grooming and uniform standards, the sense of tactical awareness—those are personal strategies established and ingrained during military service.

Early in my corporate experience, I was at a breakfast meeting with my direct supervisor and several other people. We were already seated, eating at the table, before the CEO arrived. As the CEO walked up, I reflexively stood—not quite to attention. That's what you do in the military when your commander approaches. About halfway to vertical, I caught every eye at the table turning to me, and they chuckled nervously and urged me to sit down. It's a funny example, but the way that response was ingrained in me demonstrates how retired military personnel have trained their brains and bodies to react without thinking —these systems take time to recalibrate. It also offers a small insight into why some may struggle to adjust to corporate culture.

When I work with corporate clients, I can usually pick out the employees who are former military personnel. Some services might soften a bit more after retirement, but the bearing and heart of the connection to service never change. Many retired military members settle into roles that seem to duplicate their last military assignment. In my experience, and without stereotyping too much, former Navy Seals are often very tactical in business, and that's their sweet spot. When they come into a corporate setting, they tend to view the problems from a tactical perspective and want to be hands-on. This is not a methodology that always works in the long term.

In corporate life, senior leaders can forget how to get their hands dirty. They often reach a point where they forget they can learn more. It's common to observe a retired senior military leader in a corporate role expect that a meeting will be conducted with the same discipline as meetings on active duty. By this I mean the discipline associated with a hierarchical organization, the expectation that positional leadership will carry the day. It will not. Former service members have a vast store of ingrained knowledge about leadership. However, this knowledge doesn't always transfer directly to life after service. You have to develop organizational awareness that fits your current situation and learn to adapt prior experiences to this new environment.

In uniform, we tend to recognize someone's sum of talent within weeks or months of arrival at a duty station. By contrast, when I began working in corporate, a colleague actually shared that not much is expected from you in the first year. It was well recognized that someone transitioning from active duty won't move the revenue needle immediately. But into the second year, there should be identifiable results. It seemed a pretty low bar of expectations. I took the counsel in stride.

Some of my corporate seniors were former uniformed officers; some were not. They each operated in their unique styles. Some traits and behaviors were easier to predict than others. All required consideration. Teammates would not always see things the same way as the boss or bosses. I learned from working with Army officers on the Joint Staff that it's part of their culture to lead two levels down. They have a system in place to actively reach down two levels to recruit, train and mentor people. This happens to some extent in all military branches but more formally in the Army. In corporate, there are typically no such systems in place.

Understanding that you are facing an entirely different culture after service is vital. Former military members have a different concept of what time means than their corporate counterparts. In a corporation, it is not unusual to move from one meeting to the next—just talking—for an entire eight-hour workday. In the Army they call this a BOGSAT, which stands for "Bunch of Guys Sitting around a Table," and it is avoided at all costs unless there's a real issue to be dealt with or understood. A BOGSAT can be positive if it's got a meaningful purpose. A BOGSAT without purpose is "a BOGSAT"—not productive. It requires an enormous level of tact and diplomacy to navigate leadership roles without a formal structure in place. Even the very "best places to work," as highlighted on numerous annual lists, have challenges with keeping people fulfilled and all rowing in the same direction.

During a particularly challenging period in my corporate role, I was struggling to read the leadership tea leaves; I thought I'd read up on "leading up." There are many books, some even bestsellers, about how to lead one's boss. I was looking for insight, so I thought I would study the topic and try to figure out what I was missing. It didn't take more than the first couple of chapters to recognize the problem.

It wasn't my boss at all. It was me.

I was misguided in thinking I was going to change, steer, redirect or otherwise lead my boss. What needed to change was me. I needed to accept that I was the one fitting into an organization, not the other way around. I was grappling with culture but wasn't sure why.

The risk was missing, the well-defined mission. Nobody was even expecting me to move the needle. It was up to me to adjust. I was accustomed to clear directives, core values and shared ideology. I lost my sense of SA, and the understanding of the big picture of the company was not as clear to me as it could and should have been. The responsibilities, loyalties and accountabilities across the company could change regularly.

Confiding in colleagues from other companies has confirmed for me that this type of transition struggle is common. When I expressed dissatisfaction with the ambiguity of corporate structure, "Get used to it" and "they're paying you a lot, just put up with it" were typical responses.

My misguided attempt to "fix my boss" should have been a signal that I needed to stop and check my light list because I was off course.

Unfortunately, I proceeded to adapt for a couple more years. In retrospect, it was wasted time. My compensation and quality of life were enviable, but the fulfillment from the work was low. I should have moved on.

There is no substitute for a higher purpose. Political maneuvering involves self-interest, conforming and manipulating for the desired outcome so that your position wins. Whereas diplomacy is the example of Senator McCain, Senator Lieberman or Senator Bill Nelson. Each had a higher purpose to their work.

As a senator for Florida, Nelson took responsibility to tune into Central and South America because his constituency was impacted by issues of the region. His actions weren't about him; they were to understand the issues. On one of our diplomatic trips, I remember walking through a sugarcane field that had been decimated by deforestation. Nelson could have asked for a few days to visit Machu Picchu for "cultural awareness" but chose the more challenging issues to focus on. That was not a comfortable trip to make. Our challenges included a small plane, significant changes in the altitude of countries visited in short succession and full schedules, but Nelson chose to walk the field guided by his higher purpose to serve.

Based on the master-level diplomacy lessons I learned in service, I am able to go toe-to-toe with leaders of companies I serve today. It's a fine line, but you must be your own arbiter of good taste—timing is the essence of diplomacy. There are times when everyone doesn't agree on the best decision. That can be okay. There are also times when the only point of consensus is that the decision doesn't need to be made today. In some cases, a clear solution will present itself to some people but not to others. There is no reason to attack or approach differences of opinion aggressively.

Competence carries the day. To lead effectively, you have to know what you're talking about. You can't be searching on Google for what something means. You must own the material to have conversations at those senior levels. That's why Nelson needed to walk through the sugarcane field himself. The common thread that runs through all acts of diplomacy is confidence. It's why McCain, Lugar, Kyl and Lieberman knew they had to be on the ground, face to face with the situation. The good news is you can develop competence to build your confidence. You can at least become proficient enough to convey expertise with a minimal amount of effort. Even the most toxic leaders can be tempered when someone can stand up to them with facts.

In entrepreneurship, diplomacy means being equipped to handle the fact that sometimes clients will not apply your advice. They have the power to do that, but facts will always win if you have the courage and awareness to carry them to the right setting. To preserve relationships, you must master timing, level-headedness and diplomacy.

9

UNDERSTAND ORGANIZATIONS

"Understand who controls your bonus—that's your real boss." -GM

Every Navy organization has a SORM. This acronym stands for "standard organization and regulation manual." It's a book outlining how each ship is organized that serves as a tool to help keep ships' operations homogenous. The SORM serves as a common guide that is then tailored more specifically to each set of circumstances. The very concept of a SORM allows for those in service to move from one organization to another within the Navy with a pretty good feel for how a unit is organized and how responsibilities and authorities are divided.

I have yet to see something as exhaustive as a SORM in business. Companies often have procedures and internal levels of organization in place, but they don't typically translate as exactly as a SORM from one facility to the next.

In my consulting work, I'm inspired by the concept of the SORM. I like to apply a SORM framework to help my clients. Identifying the mission and responsibilities for a company starts by helping the leaders answer the question, "How do I (fill in the blank)?" I've learned that understanding why is more important than how. Many are searching for how before they have figured out why. I notice common threads in their answers include recognizing how to apply operations, remove limitations and find new ways forward.

My background allows me to speak the language of military operations but also the language of Washington, DC. Clients I work with sometimes have parts of either language covered but need help actually communicating their story. Recognizing I could speak these multiple languages has served me well, as it has my clients. I fundamentally recognize that the government customer is often working with its version of a SORM of which my clients might not be aware. The concept applies to most agencies of government; I help clients understand the organization as much as I help them understand the process they are selling into.

My knowledge of both organizations and process helps a company do what needs to be done faster than their competitor. It's much like coordinating operations: you don't need to do it all, but you must do what's important at the right time and place.

I will never forget preparing for my first command in 1999. A trusted admiral, John Harvey, who would later rise to four stars, gave me counsel.

He said to me, "As commander, you just need to get your ship to the right place at the right time and have at least one radio that works."

He was only half-joking. Of course, today's ships have dozens of communications options. I could pick up a handset on my desk and have a dial tone for a phone call. But it can still be a struggle to be on the right channel at the right place and time. His point was to stay focused, but so much goes into that.

I took a trip to Mexico with my family in 2007 while I was contemplating retirement from service. I had recently failed to select as admiral on my first "early" look, and this caused a fundamental shift in my direction. Up until that point, my Navy career had maintained consistent forward momentum, and this lack of promotion was significant. Many who had served in my position over the years had gone on to select for flag—I had served with them. I also knew the process of promotions at this level of the Navy and how admirals were assigned their jobs from my early exposure in flag officer detailing. The overwhelming number of the most senior flag officers select into the flag community early or on the first "regular" look. My keenly developed sense of SA told me that once you lose momentum, it's difficult to get it back. Several seniors would suggest I wait for the next look but had observed too many staying on active duty too long, hoping for that next promotion. On that trip, I had time to reflect on the global perspective of the Navy I spent two decades acquiring.

I understood the Navy as an organization, but I also spent my entire adult life to that point in service to the higher purpose of the Navy. This made the decision to retire both personal and professional. I spent quite a bit of time considering my options and weighing pros and cons. Finally, I found a three-by-five card and started making a list. By then, the concept of the light list was more than a nautical tool: it was a proven method for keeping things straight that I had successfully adapted to my own life many times.

On that index card, I created a light list of targets for my remaining working years. I knew logically that my chances of selecting for admiral decreased with each look and, with that understanding, I recognized the opportunity in front of me. I challenged myself to think of reasons why I should wait and try again when I could retire from the Navy with many good earning years still ahead of me. In that moment, I looked at my service for the first time from the point of view of a careerist. This was a signal of the fundamental shift in my thinking. While the Navy is a career, being a careerist is not what the Navy is about.

I listed our four daughters' ages, calculating the approximate number of years they each had left at home, factoring in the monetary cost of college tuition, cars, weddings and the other trappings of young adulthood. Beyond the monetary amounts, I considered the amount of time spent away from my family and the things I loved if I were to commit to a military schedule of traveling, commuting and sitting in meetings. I looked at the number of years our daughters had left at home and the number of years I had left to work; I considered our savings, assets, cost of living and calculated approximately what we would need to make the whole equation work.

Now, more than a decade later, I wish I still had that index card. I know for certain that my corporate earnings blew all my proposed plans and profits out of the water within the first few years. But far beyond the financial success I found in corporate, my decision to pursue entrepreneurship has afforded me irreplaceable time with my family and inspiration for personal growth beyond my wildest dreams. No index card can capture those intangibles.

In command, I was leading a ship but also fulfilling a role in a larger organization. The ship was just one element of a battle group in some cases. In other situations, the ship might have been the sole representation of US resolve visiting a country, sitting off the coast of another country or operating in a multinational force. The influence of the ship varied based on its role within an environment. As such, my role would adapt as well.

Later, as I prepared to retire from the Navy in 2008, I paid a visit to my former senior, Vice Admiral Cutler Dawson. He had recently retired from service after 34 years and was the CEO of Navy Federal Credit Union, the largest credit union in the world. He served in that role for 14 years, growing the organization exponentially in membership, branches and assets. He also knew my background, so I particularly valued his input as I prepared to embark on the next phase of my career.

Dawson was amiable as always; he made some observations about our time working together and offered to make a few introductions for me. Then he asked a question I will never forget.

He leaned back in his chair and looked at me: "Have you ever considered becoming a lobbyist?"

I remembered my congressional fellowship in 2003, where I discovered I was positioned to see the big picture and I possessed the unique skillset of helping others do the same. Until that point, I had never considered legislative work after the Navy. Now it was time to give it some thought. Dawson's recommendation and the introductions he offered played a role in my decision-making process.

During my time in Washington, DC, I had become an avid listener of Radio Margaritaville, Jimmy Buffett's satellite radio station. The long commutes to DC gave me plenty of time to tune in. Even today, all my vehicles stay tuned to Sirius channel 24. During a long drive one day, as I contemplated retirement from the service and weighed my options, I caught a live version of the song "Volcano" and an interview with Jimmy Buffett. I will always have a soft spot for that song since my adventure on the island of Montserrat during my first deployment.

During the interview, Jimmy Buffett laughingly pointed out that the song, which involves repeating the words "I don't know" over and over, essentially has very simple lyrics. He said something like, "It's one of my favorites, but it only has three words and three chords. Hey—not everything good has to be complicated."

This idea gave me pause. Jimmy Buffett is one of the wealthiest musicians in the world. He built a multi-million-dollar empire on just a few lyrics and chords on a guitar. I saw him from an operational perspective then, recognizing his unique skillset translated to many different projects, too many for me to count. As I had observed his career over the decades, I watched him reinvent himself from the barefoot guitarist, playing for 50 people on the dock in Key West, to an international superstar, bestselling author, restaurateur and a resort developer. He continued to write and play music, touring every year with his loyal Parrotheads.

His example stuck in my mind as I considered my next move. He was the captain of his empire, responsible for owning and growing his brand. He found a way to achieve success, build his business and maintain his vision.

Not everything good has to be complicated; just ask Jimmy Buffett.

* * *

In entrepreneurship, you create your own organizational structure. There is no SORM. Therefore, it is important to maintain a growth mindset and invest in yourself with a conceptual SORM in mind. This can take several forms, and I don't pretend to have the prescription for everyone. The truth is, we each need to tailor our own training program.

When I chose not to pursue another corporate job and got serious about consulting, I began by reading books. I thought I understood consulting, having hired several consultants and observed dozens in action over the years. By complete chance, a colleague suggested a book by Alan Weiss called *Getting Started in Consulting*. It was a remarkable read that quickly opened my eyes to how much I didn't know about consulting. Sadly, it also confirmed the limited view shared by nearly every consultant I had previously come in contact with.

There's a reason Alan is number one in the world in this space.

Around the same time, another colleague had suggested the value I might get from an "executive coach." I met with one over coffee. It was a curious meeting where he attempted to identify "which wall I should place my ladder on." I was 50 years old. I found the conversation ridiculous and could sense his desperation to land a new client. I wasn't ready. I wasn't open. Unfortunately for him as well, he wasn't ready—or able —to move me to a new understanding of how I might benefit from his counsel.

I had already found the guide I needed to create my own organization. The coach hadn't figured out he was in desperate need of one.

The "Million Dollar Consultant," Alan Weiss is a prolific author and the recognized global leader in coaching consultants of all stripes around the globe. I quickly read several of his books and began applying his concepts as I began consulting and landing clients. As I engaged with prospects, generated referrals and moved to written proposals, I found Weiss's methods and descriptions to be practical and highly effective. It took me a couple years to invest more fully in his live teaching events. I should not have waited. What his work brought back for me was filling the void of learning I was experiencing in a corporate headquarters job. It took me a while to realize that the lack of fulfillment was largely attributable to the fact that I wasn't growing professionally.

I thought to myself, "How could I have not seen this world of possibilities sooner?"

I believe this fundamental awakening is critical for

every member of the military to understand as they transition beyond active duty.

Here's the trick. Break out your highlighter. You must spend some money on yourself to experience high-quality learning and training. The business-building version of you must spend money to make money. Spending is not something military people do readily or extravagantly. Listen up. There is a difference between spending and investing in yourself. I have invested thousands on such high-caliber training.

It has allowed me to learn how to apply my skills fully and make millions. They go hand in hand.

In 2019 I decided to write my first book. It was something that I had never given serious thought. However, as I learned about building a business, I discovered books enhance public credibility. As I set out to outline the book, I realized the material had been accumulating in my brain for decades. The experiences I was sharing anecdotally with clients could have broader appeal to a larger audience in need of assistance. Many companies don't fully understand federal budgeting and appropriations, and that lack of knowledge inhibits their sales. I recognized I could reach more people by writing a book that simplified the federal funding and buying process. My highly capable intern at the time, Caroline Gelinne, helped me put together a credible manuscript in a few months' time.

The final phase of the manuscript was completed while Julie and I were exploring the Bahamas in our boat. The last time we had been in the Bahamas together, we stayed in Freeport for a three-day, two-night honeymoon in 1984. We could only make that trip because my new status as a Navy ensign qualified me for a green American Express card, and we both knew the bill was due within 30 days. Touring the islands on our own boat seemed a perfect representation of how my work lifestyle has transformed in just a few years from the intensity of military service to the freedom to create my own organization. As if to put icing on the cake, I landed a client during that trip as well. I have long since confirmed clients don't care where I am geographically, as long as I'm available to help and deliver on our agreed objectives.

In my consulting work, I have expanded my networks far beyond the defense industry that I primarily serve. I now have ongoing outreach and support from a global network of consultants who work in all sorts of industries and situations worldwide. I actively work to maintain a global perspective on issues far outside my daily work routine. Those experiences and everything I am describing help differentiate me from would-be consulting peers in my government relations space.

When the pandemic really took hold, many scrambled to figure out remote work. Some were slow on the uptake. Some never quite figured it out. I had already built this framework for my business. I had been doing it successfully for years, having witnessed colleagues outside the military and defense establishment doing it for quite some time. I believe the investment of my time and effort to learn effective techniques for remote work uniquely positioned me to thrive during the pandemic in 2020.

10

TAKE OWNERSHIP

"Give serious thought to how long you want to work. Some are clinging to a dated notion of what retirement is, what it could be or what it should be for them." -GM

A Navy captain is fully responsible for command of the ship. This is a cultural dynamic that has been developed over centuries. The US Navy largely adopted this practice from the Royal Navy. This sense of ownership can become overbearing or intrusive. If there is some faulty cultural dynamic that is seeping into the workplace, it should be a concern for the leadership team. In corporate America, there is often no system for oversight of the culture created by middle managers. It's nobody's business. Unless you choose to go to your boss about it.

In the military, command ownership *can* apply to personal things, but it is meant to apply to procedural things. If you can't communicate on the radio channels, if your ship is not where it is supposed to be or not functioning, that's your problem. That sense of complete ownership is very well understood in the Navy and applies in the other services, too.

There is less leeway for slacking off in the Navy than in the corporate world. When the work is equally divided, those who are not pulling their weight are weeded out over time. In the corporate setting, it's typically up to those with experience to help people in the corporate environment to see how their choices impact the company. I have talked to people who are not happy in their corporate job because they're not in the right fit. The cultures are different, the pressures are different and the units of measurement are different.

In the military culture, you own the whole sailor.

When I commanded a ship, if I learned that a sailor and his wife were having domestic problems and the police had been called, I was allowed to order that sailor not to go home for a very specific period. This is called a military protection order. I gave a couple of these orders during my two command tours. I can't imagine having that degree of connection and involvement in someone else's life choices in any other circumstances. My motivation was not just protecting the sailor and their family; it was a larger responsibility to the higher purpose of the Navy and our country. There is no handbook that teaches judgment and common sense. You don't learn those things in captain class.

"Ownership" of the people in corporate does not translate like this.

Military service instills a deep sense of ownership and responsibility for the United States. We carry this sense of higher purpose throughout our lives, even after retirement.

All military members who have completed deployments to other countries can relate to the sensations associated with returning home to US soil (or waters). For most, the anticipation of returning home from overseas brings about strong feelings of anticipation and excitement.

Each service, and the community or branch within each service, has traditions associated with return to home port or home base. Fireboat tugs, draping the bow of a ship with a lei made by the families and bands on the pier are just a few examples common in the Navy.

For ships returning from sea, it's common to top off on fuel alongside an oiler before coming into port the next day. It's generally believed refueling at sea is easier and involves less risk of spill than refueling in port. When ships refuel from an oiler, they steam alongside each other just over 100 feet apart, at a speed of about 13 knots. During this time, they are connected by fuel hoses and transfer hundreds of thousands of gallons of fuel very quickly. Upon completion of refueling, the newly refueled ship will "break away" from the receiving ship.

It's common practice for the commander to allow

their crew to choose a "break away" song to blast from the ship's topside sound system as it returns to top speed approaching home port. Throughout my years in service, I came to recognize this transition as the final stretch on the light list for each journey. It was always a powerful moment for me.

I have a vivid recollection of the breakaway song at the culmination of a six-month deployment.

It wasn't Jimmy Buffett. Our ship voted to play Motley Crüe's "Home Sweet Home" as the breakaway song that day. I recall that I didn't know it off the top of my head, but it was the song they chose.

Even for a Parrothead, the power of that song is universal. It perfectly captures the effort put forth to prepare for a deployment, the tenacity required to persist and succeed and how the final return home doesn't just happen for any of us. It takes a lot of work, preparation and testing throughout. To this day, if I hear Motley Crüe's "Home Sweet Home" or play it in the car, it takes me back to that specific feeling of having completed a successful deployment and the imminent return to home.

In the early days following a return from deployment, beyond the return to my family, I was always struck with an intense recognition of how abundant, different and downright lucky we are to live in the US. We have freedom of choice, freedom of movement and freedom of decision like no other country. I believe that as we mature, the sensation of overwhelm at the sheer choice we live with and often take for granted every day begins to fade. I think this is because we feel a need to simplify and compartmentalize in order to make sense of our daily lives in a complex world.

I encourage you to close your eyes and reflect on your own "Home Sweet Home" experience. Allow yourself to once again internalize the promise and the hope, the incredible satisfaction that comes from personal and team accomplishments in service to a higher cause.

After reflecting on that for a minute or two, look around at your present professional circumstances. Ask yourself some questions: Are you where you should be? Are you accepting something less than you deserve just because it's within reach? Are you applying yourself the way you did on deployment? What's next on your light list? How will your life look different one, three or five years down the road?

For too many of us, the answer is, "It won't." Don't let that happen to you.

* * *

Ownership in corporate has a different feeling—people go home at the end of the day. If someone was having a hard time personally, often the issue is avoided for fear of an HR concern. At least on the part of the employee. On a ship, the command master chief (senior-most enlisted person on the ship) could come in and tell me there was an issue and that I might need to send someone home for a while. This would likely lead to a private conversation with the sailor in my cabin where we decide together if they should go spend some time at home. That dynamic doesn't exist in corporate. That level of ownership over an employee might appear intrusive.

Nothing but experience can teach you how to interpret situations.

As a military person in a corporate setting, I was paid a lot of money for just muddling. It's a common condition. It took me a few years to recognize this because moving to the corporate world from service, the money was better than I had ever seen, so I assumed it was what I was supposed to do for the good of my family. I had more flexibility, I was home more often and the family was satisfied. But I was missing fulfillment that can only come from a higher purpose.

I'm a classic lone wolf as described by many management books. I had learned to work within the context of a crew but thrived in command due to the autonomy inherent in the role. It's not great to be a lone wolf in corporate. It's not ideal to be a lone wolf as a member of the ship's crew. But life as a consultant is the land of the lone wolf. I have learned to thrive using my skillset, organizational savvy and self-discipline to determine the needs a company cannot see or implement for itself. Those feelings of responsibility and accountability are natural to me.

I once had a mentor tell me, "The title of command should fit you like a well-tailored suit—you can tell when someone is not a good fit in the role as captain." Translated to corporate: "Empty suits are easy to find in Washington."

Entrepreneurship has its own set of responsibilities. It's all about self-assessment, self-awareness and self-value. It's about jumping ahead to build the positive aspects that come with this sense of ownership. It's learning how to be a better consultant, to communicate better, keep up with technology, be attuned to strategy and corporate concerns. If people don't see value in me, they're not going to hire me. I know my own value and can bring a lifetime of experiences and solutions to the specific challenges my clients are facing.

I am like a lighthouse that can guide their path.

I'm the guy who understands their position, their goals and what we need to avoid. These high-stakes communicating skills were developed in my own service and sharpened during my personal development after military retirement. Today, I can convey that solution set to clients who are struggling during transitions or experiencing unsettled periods.

After watching some superb public speakers like Colleen Francis and Connie Dieken live, I recognized I needed to up my game in public speaking. In the military, what we consider public speaking is really presenting. There's a difference. Highly effective public speakers can grab audiences with emotion and stories while instantly conveying credibility and professionalism. It's very different than watching a military leader present. I invested in this shortcoming and, as such, have become even better at conveying details in memorable ways. That only happened because I made the personal investment in learning to do it better.

I never used to envision myself walking into the Pentagon, selling for a company. Now I recognize that no matter where you go, you're going to be selling. I don't roam the halls of federal buildings to sell, but there is no doubt that I do sell both my services and my clients' solutions and capabilities. That is the nature of a capitalist marketplace. Again, investing in learning about the science and art behind selling required a touch of humility and a willingness to pay for professional help.

Today I sell my capabilities and support others on my own terms. I don't have any long-term contracts in place. All my work arrangements are made with a two-page proposal outlining objectives, metrics, a timeline and terms. That puts pressure on me to deliver ongoing value and gives the client an escape hatch by not having a long-term obligation. It squarely puts the responsibility on me to over-deliver. This takes a certain amount of self-confidence, but I have worked hard to hone the competence and the underlying skills. Clients see value and retain me over the long term. Like command, I am comfortable with being completely accountable.

Committing to my own growth allowed me to let go

of the fear of stepping out on my own that often holds others back. I apply everything I know to make high-stakes decisions. If I let a high-value client go because they don't behave as we had agreed or their technology turns out to be of no interest to the government, that loss of income is real and immediate to me, but those are the rules of this game.

Focusing on properly screening prospective clients and then delivering value fuels my confidence that I am very much an expert in my field. Fear doesn't hold me back because I've taught myself that fear in my business is not rational. There is a resilience that I have developed, but it's born of self-confidence and an absence of fear. This requires a sense of ownership. This is not a superhuman skill—it exists in most people; they just don't use it.

Upon leaving the Navy, Julie and I further explored our enthusiasm for boats with variants of increasing size, capability and levels of performance. The family yacht we own today is known as a Pilot House Explorer, a semi-displacement hull that measures just under 50 tons. I believe my Navy skills serve me well in the pleasure boating to which I was first introduced in my teens.

As we began to explore further reaches, including open water passages, I recognized the limitations of us running the boat as a couple. Although my Navy career led me to command of ships, command of a ship is not the same as running a boat offshore. Navy ships have highly trained crews and the best equipment available for emergencies.

The smallest ship I served on was a frigate that displaced roughly 4,000 tons. The destroyer and cruiser I commanded displaced roughly 9,000 tons. They are ships of substantial size and proportion. Docking and undocking a ship that size is much like moving a building from its position on a city block. It is done slowly and carefully. Maneuvering alongside an oiler to take on fuel, with both ships moving at 13 knots and separated by just 120 feet, also must be done deliberately and in accordance with a process.

During my Navy training, I was regularly trained and certified to a competency standard. Selection to command takes multiple forms, including promotion to rank, administrative board selection, oral board performance, completion of coursework and of course demonstration of ship handling skills along the way.

Ironically, Navy credentials don't automatically translate to recognized maritime credentials of the Coast Guard. This is changing as of this writing, but my Navy time at sea did not directly translate to Coast Guard licensing. Having a Coast Guard captain's license is not required to operate pleasure boats, as long as your insurance company approves. Our insurance company accepts my nautical experience at sea for what it is— years at sea.

During Florida hurricane season, owners are often in search of qualified captains to relocate their boats. It is the civilian equivalent of the exodus I experienced in 1989 to get every operational boat out of port as Hurricane Hugo bore down on Charleston. We have lived this experience personally, and I have a soft spot for boat owners who are snowbirds or must evacuate and leave their boats in an uncertain predicament. After several years of witnessing this, it occurred to me that maybe helping move these boats would be something fun to do as a side gig down the road. When I did some initial research, I discovered, alas, for a third party such as me to move a substantial-sized boat, USCG credentialing is generally required.

During this same period, my many experiences at sea generated a nagging feeling about the ever-present risks of operating our boat with a two-person crew offshore. I recognized I could stand to sharpen my skills. My respect for the ocean learned as a teen, and honed through a Navy career, allowed me to see the need for ongoing training. Since leaving active duty, my performance at sea is no longer formally observed and critiqued by others. However, I understand how to self-assess. This is a skillset most military service members also possess. Based on my own assessment, my sense of responsibility as an owner and a captain inspired action.

With these factors motivating me, I went back to "Sea School" in 2019 to qualify for the certification as a 200-ton level USCG captain. More than a decade after my retirement from the Navy, I humbled myself to recognize I could use the refresher. I collected the required documentation of experience, attended the classroom sessions, completed the practical examinations and independently earned the certification. Most Florida boaters possess no such training. It's simply not required.

In attaining the credential, I became a "captain, captain," US Navy and US Coast Guard! I can't help but recall that Captain Jim referred to himself as a "captain, captain," US Navy and the commercial airline industry. In my role as the owner of a large boat and a retired Navy captain, I identified a knowledge gap. I became a USCG captain for myself and the safety of my wife. For me, this was a signal of both personal and professional growth.

11

EMBRACE GROWTH

"People die. You will as well. Don't assume you've got decades ahead of you." -GM

After taking the three career paths of military, corporate and entrepreneurship, one of my biggest moments of self-discovery was the day I realized real fulfillment happens when you know you are growing. In the military, you're continually being prepared for the next big thing; you go back to school, refresh certifications and build new skillsets. Training and preparation are constant in the military. After you retire, you have to create some of that self-improvement activity or otherwise find a way to associate with it.

This concept of investing in oneself is likely my biggest learning point since leaving active duty. I know several executive coaches who coach people individually. Executive coaching is a cottage industry—but this kind of support is available if you know where to look. It is shocking to me that it's typically managed through the HR department and is available to only a select few.

Some of those coaches can cost tens of thousands, which is steep but within reach for many. It amazes me that most senior VPs won't spend money on that kind of support for themselves. It's a failure to invest. They might work on an advanced degree if the company is paying. An MBA at Georgetown might cost $75K. Many executives can afford to self-fund that investment but won't. I don't see people doing it with their own dollar when they could (and should). I look at continuing my education and maintaining a growth mindset as a cost of doing business because if I don't, I am going to get steamrolled.

Too many people in the business world become confined by a job description. They mistakenly think the static job description for which they were hired is their only option. In fact, that job description was likely drafted by HR, then run through Legal. Supervisors probably identified desirable characteristics and traits for the candidate. They provide the definition and do the skills tests, but once you're in, all bets are off. Now you need to adapt to your environment and identify how you can best help in that environment and grow.

* * *

I believe those with prior military service often possess enormous untapped potential.

Service offers all members a framework for success, but learning to apply those lessons takes effort. I hope my personal examples of adapting to new situations during service will remind you of your own hard-won lessons in courage, leadership and diplomacy. After retirement from service, you must draw on your senses of situational awareness and discernment to create your own light list. Blooming where planted has certainly worked for me time after time. But after military service, *you really can choose where you want to plant yourself.*

Recognizing the value of consistently investing in my personal growth has opened doors and opportunities that were unimaginable to me as I left the Navy. Your experiences have value, just as mine do. Yours will be different. Don't make a literal comparison to the stories I've shared or the path I have chosen. Take your own inventory. Press the boundaries of your present circumstances. Identify how you may be self-editing your own dreams. Is it possible, even just a little, that fear is keeping you from doing something different?

Here's a test. If someone handed you a million dollars with no strings attached, what would you do with it? Would you relocate? Quit your job? Buy something? Start a business? Contribute more to charity? You don't have to wait for the magical million dollars to appear to do any of those things. But you might need to change your thinking about why you aren't doing those things now.

I hope this book inspires you to think more clearly about how you move beyond your transition. We all deserve to work for professional fulfillment and a higher purpose, and it may look different for you than your peers. The military community is remarkably small, yet for many of us, it can consume our identity—even after our active service is complete. You don't have to simply follow a course laid out before you. This amazing country allows you to write, edit and rewrite your light list.

Look for inspiration as you chart your own course. Perspective is a gift: allow yourself to use it.

As I navigated transitions in my own life, I found myself following the examples of those I admired—like my dad, my Uncle Jack and Captain Jim. As I explored the world and found new opportunities, I encountered powerful lessons that guided me. John Ruehlin's military transition course made an impact on me early in my service and has served as an ongoing inspiration. As I advanced in the Navy, I encountered respected seniors like Admirals Cutler Dawson and Steve Abbot, as well as Generals Lloyd Austin and Greg Newbold, who demonstrated advanced leadership talents that directed and illuminated my path. Working with Senators Lieberman, Luger, Kyl, Nelson and McCain, who embodied the very best qualities of elected officials, demonstrated the higher purpose of the US in action. After retirement,

I drew from these foundational experiences to grow my own way. Connecting with Alan Weiss has been instrumental in my transition to consulting, and he continues to serve as a mentor.

And then there's Jimmy Buffett.

Jimmy Buffett is a guiding light that has remained consistent in my life for decades. His music has always embodied the life of sailing and sun on the Florida coast that I embraced as a teen and was drawn back to after retirement from the Navy. As I grew up, I followed his career and learned personal stories the way fans do. He sings and tells the story that his parents wanted him to be a priest or a naval officer, but he chose to support himself by playing guitar. He built that passion into an empire and has navigated many of his own life transitions in the public eye. He has continued to grow and reinvent himself, from a barefoot guitarist to a mogul who uses his resources and creativity to build communities and give back.

Giving back is my goal with this book. I hope I inspire you to think creatively about how you will make the most of your years after military service. Giving something back also guides many of my decisions at this stage of my life. I embrace chances to connect my life experiences to causes that I feel passionate about. One such cause is a nonprofit called Freedom Fighter Outdoors that creates unique outdoor experiences for injured service members and veterans, including boating, hunting and sport fishing. I learned firsthand in the

Navy that sometimes the injuries service members carry are invisible, which drew me to this organization. I met the FFO founder, Captain Vinnie LaSorsa, through a professional colleague in the leisure marine community. I greatly admire Captain Vinnie's skills and commitment to the higher purpose of the organization.

When I later discovered Jimmy Buffett is also a big supporter of the organization, it was another signal to guide my path. As I wrote this book, I was inspired to donate the proceeds to help former service members through FFO. It is an honor to be supporting such a worthy cause in the good company of one of my heroes.

My work, in and out of the Navy, illuminated for me the need for highly committed people to serve our nation both in uniform and government. Recognizing that sometimes people need a little help to pursue a passion for working in government, Julie and I endowed a perpetual scholarship at our alma mater, Florida State University. Its express purpose is to offer financial support to motivated students pursuing master's-level education in public policy with a desire to work in government. My exposure to some of the great American leaders of our time has convinced me that we need more people in government who are guided by a higher purpose.

Although I feel lucky to have learned from great military and business leaders, my more recent experiences with global online learning have also exposed me to remarkable people we may never see on the news.

My pursuit of a PhD involved earning a master's of philosophy in public policy and administration. In my virtual classroom, I met students from all over the world. I was shocked to learn adults in West African nations were keeping up with our rigorous coursework, using shared devices in an internet café to connect to the classroom. In some cases, English is their second or even third language. I was immediately struck by that level of determination, even in the face of far less immediate opportunity.

Those international students were working far harder than I was to improve their condition. They have fewer advantages than any of us who have served in the United States Armed Forces. We live in a remarkable country that affords incredible opportunity. Pursue your postmilitary career with the hunger, energy and passion of some of my classmates. This is your life—you are not completing a checklist of the next set of requirements or inspections.

Look upon your service with pride, but don't let it define your remaining working years. Maintain your commitment to growth no matter where your path takes you. How many years did you determine that you have? Make them count.

Don't wait. Make your move.

ACKNOWLEDGMENTS

The predicate for this book was an incredibly fulfilling career in the United States Navy. Throughout my Navy career, I was immersed in one of our nation's greatest leadership laboratories filled with the best people our country produces. I remain grateful for the countless shipmates with whom I was privileged to serve.

My wife, Julie, our four daughters, and our growing family of sons and grandchildren have been an ongoing source of love and support without which this evolving story would not be possible.

Becky Sasso, who brought these words to life, and the entire team at Launch Pad Publishing kept this passion project on track and made it the reality it was meant to be.

The inspiration of great people like Vinnie and Sarah LaSorsa and their work leading Freedom Fighter Outdoors gave this book its real meaning.

ABOUT THE AUTHOR

Gene Moran transitioned from the Navy in 2008 as a captain after 24 years of service, commanding ships and advising senior leaders. He spent five years in a corporate role before recognizing his lack of fulfillment for what it was—a failure to invest in himself. Moran subsequently transitioned to a new adventure in entrepreneurship as founder and president of his consulting firm, Capitol Integration.

In 2020, Moran's work as a consultant was recognized for excellence by his industry peers when he was named a Top Lobbyist by the National Institute for Lobbying and Ethics and recognized by the Society for Advancing Consulting with the Corrie Shanahan Memorial Award for Advancing Consulting. In 2021 Moran was inducted into the Million Dollar Consulting Hall of Fame®, and his firm, Capitol Integration, was identified as a Top Lobbying Firm by Bloomberg Government, one of few solo-practitioners so recognized.

Moran maintains a working presence in Washington, DC, but resides in sunny Florida with his wife, Julie, and their boats. He completed licensing to become a 200-ton Masters-level USCG Captain and is currently pursuing a PhD in Public Policy and Administration.